IT'S MY TURN

20 KINGDOM LABORERS WHO CHANGED THEIR WORLD AND COMPEL ME TO IMPACT MINE!

FORGE

© 2020 by Forge. All rights reserved.

Published by Forge, 14485 East Evans Avenue, Denver, Colorado 80014

Unless otherwise stated, Scripture quotations are taken from the Holy Bible, New International Version® NIV® Copyright © 1973, 1978, 1984 by International Bible Society. Used by Permission of Zondervan. All rights reserved.

No portion of this publication may be reproduced, stored in a retrieval system, or transmitted in any other form or by any means electronic, mechanical, photocopy, recording or any other without the permission of the publisher.

Requests to use material contained in this publication should be in writing to: Publisher, Forge 14485 East Evans Avenue, Denver, Colorado 80014

Written, researched, compiled, and revised by Forge Staff 1998-2020

Visit us online at www.forgeforward.org

CONTENTS

Foreword	v
Introduction	xi

PART I
IT'S MY TURN TO LIVE WITH A HEART ON FIRE

1. Keith Green (1954-1982) — 3
   DECLARATION 1 – It's my turn to love God with passion and intentionality
2. Josiah Henson (1789-1883) — 9
   DECLARATION 2 – It's my turn to sacrificially lay down my life for God and Others
3. Florence Nightingale (1820-1910) — 15
   DECLARATION 3 – It's my turn to love and serve with humility
4. C.T. Studd (1862-1931) — 21
   DECLARATION 4 – It's my turn to say yes to God with reckless abandon
5. Luis Palau (1934–) — 27
   DECLARATION 5 – It's my turn to trust Jesus for a God-Sized vision
6. George Müller (1805-1898) — 33
   DECLARATION 6 – It's my turn to live by radical faith
7. Watchman Nee (1903-1972) — 39
   DECLARATION 7 – It's my turn to willingly suffer for the Kingdom of God
8. Amy Carmichael (1867-1951) — 45
   DECLARATION 8 – It's my turn to die to self in order to exalt Christ
9. John Hyde (1865-1912) — 51
   DECLARATION 9 – It's my turn to intercede in prayer for the spiritually lost
10. William Wilberforce (1759-1833) — 57
    DECLARATION 10 – It's my turn to persevere in life and love

PART II
IT'S MY TURN TO LIVE A LIFE ON PURPOSE

11. Susanna Wesley (1669-1742) — 65
    DECLARATION 11 – It's my turn to embrace my unique role in God's Kingdom
12. Eric Liddell (1902-1945) — 71
    DECLARATION 12 – It's my turn to use my God-given gifts for His glory
13. Martin Luther (1483-1546) — 77
    DECLARATION 13 – It's my turn to stand for God's truth

14. D.L. Moody (1837-1899) 83
    DECLARATION 14 – It's my turn to share the good news of Jesus with the lost
15. Hudson Taylor (1832-1905) 89
    DECLARATION 15 – It's my turn to go wherever God sends me
16. Jarena Lee (1783-1864) 95
    DECLARATION 16 – It's my turn to courageously embrace God's calling
17. John Paton (1824-1907) 101
    DECLARATION 17 – It's my turn to become a threat to the kingdom of darkness
18. William Booth (1829-1912) 107
    DECLARATION 18 – It's my turn to love the overlooked and undervalued
19. William Carey (1761-1834) 113
    DECLARATION 19 – It's my turn to engage the nations
20. Dawson Trotman (1906-1956) 119
    DECLARATION 20 – It's my turn to produce and multiply more Kingdom laborers

The Laborers Declaration 125
Baton Passing as a Kingdom Laborer 129
A Runner's Guide to Racing 133
Getting the Most Out of This Book 139
Group Study Tips 143
Additional Questions & Challenges to Engage 145
Bibliography 165
More Recommended Reading 167
Forge Resources & Connection 169

FOREWORD
WHAT'S A LABORER?

Traveling place to place, Jesus saw the needs of people all around Him. Moved with compassion, He turned and spoke a word to His disciples. It was His "Plan A" for meeting the needs of people everywhere. He commanded his disciples to pray for more (and here's the word) "laborers!"

"Jesus went about all the cities and villages, teaching in their synagogues and preaching the gospel of the kingdom, and healing every disease and every infirmity. When he saw the crowds, he had compassion for them, because they were harassed and helpless, like sheep without a shepherd. Then he said to his disciples, 'The harvest is plentiful, but the laborers are few; pray therefore the Lord of the harvest to send out laborers into his harvest'" (Matthew 9:35-38 RSV, emphasis mine).

It's not a high-attraction, attention-grabbing, glamorous word. Few books, songs, or messages even use this word. Still, it's the word Jesus chose.

What the world needs, Jesus said, is laborers. Common, every day, hard-working laborers. What an equal-opportunity employment plan. Jesus said the harvest is plentiful, but the laborers are few. And He

Foreword

told us to pray that God would send laborers wherever there's human need.

In short, laborers aren't just critical to God's plan for the world—they are His plan. And there is no Plan B.

Yet for years, too many Jesus followers have been focused on ministry models involving spotlights and stages filled with highly educated, impressively gifted, and extraordinarily talented people. There's been no shortage of talented musicians, dynamic speakers, best-selling authors, powerful Christian leaders, well-known pastors, and plenty of wannabes. All the while, the desperate cry and urgent need for more Kingdom laborers remains.

More "Christian celebrities" aren't the answer to the great harvest need. When the work is done, it will have been accomplished by nameless, faceless people who did what they could, where they were, with God adding His special increase to their labor. Up-close "boots on the ground" laborers in every facet and sphere of society is what this world needs. Jesus' desire is not for an up-front few, but an up-close army of everyday mobilized laborers engaging human need where the true work needs done.

You are called to be a laborer in this army. You have a significant role to play. Scripture is full of examples of those who were ordinary in the eyes of others, but whose lives made an extraordinary impact on this world. Look at those Jesus chose to be His disciples. They weren't rabbis. They weren't the most brilliant scholars or the most charismatic speakers. They were a cross-section of ordinary people—fishermen, a tax collector, some businessmen—the kind of ordinary people Jesus still uses.

You might be wondering how a laborer is defined in the whole of Scripture. A laborer is a disciple in action. Whereas the word disciple implies one who accepts a teaching and learns from a master, the word laborer takes it one step further, implying that this teaching is put into action.

Becoming a laborer, however, isn't just about action. It's also about being in a love relationship with Jesus. Before the book of Acts reveals Peter as "a disciple in action," Peter was asked by Jesus three times,

"Do you love me?" In fact, the Bible seems to identify at least three characteristics that are hallmarks of a laborer:

Love

Laborers have an intimate love relationship with Jesus and a passion for bringing Him glory. They realize their intimacy with Jesus is the greatest gift they will ever give this world.

Life

A laborer's intimate relationship with Jesus leads to a "life of love" and acts of service often evidenced through a willingness to roll up shirt sleeves and pant legs as His laborer and wade into the mud puddles of human need where Jesus needs His laborers to be.

Legacy

Laborers leave a lasting spiritual legacy, not only through their own unique laborership, but by spiritually multiplying other Kingdom laborers like themselves. This profound baton-passing impact on people's lives is often one life at a time.

The results of these types of Kingdom laborers are eternal.

At a very young age I began reading Christian biographies. Living in a small town of just 800 people, the stories of biblical characters and other faithful Christian mentors throughout history influenced my heart and life beyond what was accessible to me in our town. These newly discovered friends and mentors became a pivotal, high-impact gift to me. My life would never be the same.

I noticed a continuum beyond the life-stories of biblical heroes of mine and recognized that God never stopped calling out ordinary people to be involved with Him in extraordinary exploits with lasting impact! All for the King, all for the Kingdom. I started calling these impactful people "Kingdom laborers." And like a drop of water in a pond, one drop causing a ripple-effect to spread out in every direction, it was clear that in the very same way one common laborer's circle of influence could be astonishingly profound. I began to imagine with Jesus an army of 24/7 laborers in all walks of life. It could become world changing.

This book is filled with awesome examples of ordinary people who simply lived with their "hearts on fire" and their "lives on purpose" as God willed and directed them daily. Notice in their lives the characteristics of a laborer. How are you being developed by God? How is He stirring within you and calling you to use your gifts in strategic ways? How does He desire His Kingdom to advance through your life as a Kingdom laborer? Are there others He wants you to focus on as a spiritually reproducing laborer?

Being near hot-hearted people is so good for us! While "hearts on fire" people may be few and far between for you in your everyday world, get ready! You are about to be among twenty people who lived so near the "all-consuming fire" of God's presence that they couldn't help but bring His heart and purposes to the world around them. Read their life-stories not to be entertained, but to be changed as you're reading. Let the Holy Spirit be near you in every page turned.

Ask yourself things like: How did God begin moving, speaking, and partnering with them? Were there special people or circumstances God used to stir their hearts or set ablaze a burden or passion within them? How did God uniquely prepare them? How long did that take? Were there sacrifices to make? Was there suffering to engage? What steps of faith were required? What spiritual gifts and character hallmarks are on display in their heart and life? Were they aware of the impact of their life? Did God open fast, miraculous windows of opportunity, or did their impact come through a long obedience in the same direction? How did God use them to spark a movement involving others? How would you sum up their ultimate life contribution?

Jesus' laborership spirit is evident in the Gospel accounts as well as in His own descriptive words, "The Son of Man came not to be served, but to serve and give His life as a ransom for many" (Mark 10:45). However, without full knowledge of God the Father's mission, Jesus' earthly family showed up one day to collect Him and take Him

Foreword

back home. They only understood His past with them in Nazareth. But Jesus, living into His future, looked at those gathered around Him and said to those also embracing God's Kingdom laborership plans and purposes for their lives, "Whoever does God's will is my brother and sister and mother" (Mark 3:35).

What happened that day? Jesus established a Kingdom lineage! He established Himself as founding Chief Cornerstone with every "living stone" fully embraced in this new Kingdom family-line. And, as Hebrews 2:11 says "Jesus is not ashamed to call them brothers and sisters." What does this mean? Your heritage is great! You belong to Jesus and all those in His Kingdom-lineage are your family members.

So, as you read these life-stories, recognize this is your Kingdom family. You are of the same Kingdom bloodline by the grace and will of God through Jesus. You have the same Father. The same Savior and Lord of the Harvest who is calling you, as He did them, to "follow me" into His spiritual harvest fields. You have the same Holy Spirit guiding you daily, empowering your life of service, and comforting you on the difficult paths of what it will take for your life to make an impact. And you can, and will, see similarities in your life and theirs across historical and generational lines.

The book You are God's Plan A…and There is No Plan B helps equip people just like you who have deeply, inwardly desired for their life to make an impact on this world. People worldwide are discovering the unique joy of living into God's powerful plans for their lives in 24/7 ordinary spaces and places of life. They're engaging ministry as distinct and unique as they are as persons. They're living into exactly what God intends for them in effectively advancing His Kingdom. So much opportunity is ahead for you!

YOU have a role to play in this extraordinary Kingdom lineage marathon. It's your turn to receive the baton from those who faithfully advanced Jesus' heart and Kingdom worldwide. At the right moment, they placed their Kingdom-advancing batons into the hands and hearts of others who would make new exchanges. It's your turn to run. You can run with confidence. You got this! How do I know? Because Jesus has you, and He will provide everything you need along the way!

Foreword

Be encouraged. No matter where you are in your spiritual journey, you can begin becoming an active Kingdom laborer right now—today. Ask God to help you share the truths and values you're capturing along the reading path of these pages, using everything you possess—from your personal social media accounts, to conversations in person or by telephone. "Sharing" information always better embosses and reinforces the important carry-forward imprint on your spirit and helps better concretize it into your own heart and life! Share quotes and benefits you're receiving with others for as long as it takes to lock those details into your memory.

Jesus, the Lord of the Harvest, who sees the needs of this world and knows you by name is calling out more Kingdom laborers to "do the works" of Him who sends them. With firm personal resolve and the passionate fire of deep conviction they're responding, "It's My Turn!"

Will you answer His call? The harvest is ripe. And by the grace, power, and ongoing calling of God, the laborers are…increasing!

Forging forward,
Dwight Robertson, Founder & CEO of *FORGE* (a praying, propagating, Kingdom laborership movement)

INTRODUCTION
WHY IS IT MY TURN NOW?

Relay races are won or lost at the handoff of the baton. Christians have continued to run the race of faith for two-thousand years now because of millions of successful baton handoffs. Jesus handed off His message of new life and Kingdom laboring to His disciples. They in turn handed the message to a few thousand believers. Those thousands gladly baton-passed the good news to the entire known world during the first century. And on and on it's gone from one generation to another.

Someone, out of love for God and love for you, handed you the message of God's love, forgiveness, and new life. Here's the question as you hold the baton in your hand: who are you going to pass it to? The only way the next generation of your family, your church, your city, your world will ever know what it means to "have life to the full" in Jesus (John 10:10) is if someone hands them the baton.

"Freely you have received," Jesus said, "freely give" (Matthew 10:8). In one way or another, the baton-passing faith runners in this book have passed the baton to you. Now, it's your turn. Future generations are counting on you. Are you ready to love God, run well, and make the pass?

A Biblical Perspective

Introduction

When God promised Abraham that his decedents would measure the number of stars in the sky, God knew that would only happen as one generation passed to the next the message of life in Yahweh.

In the fullness of time, when Jesus arrived on history's stage, His call was to "make disciples" starting close and reaching far. As Jesus stated it, "be my witnesses in Jerusalem, and in all Judea and Samaria, and to the ends of the earth" (Acts 1:8). What Jesus was calling for in fusing the "Great Commandment" (love God, love people) and "The Great Commission" (make disciples of all nations), was for generation after generation to answer the call and pass the baton of faith. Jesus established and modeled what baton-passing the good news of the gospel would look like. It would require a heart up-close to Him and a life of intentional Kingdom focus. What we refer to at Forge as having a heart on fire, life on purpose.

The Apostle Paul was among the first to help Kingdom laboring followers of Jesus put into practice daily what Jesus taught. Paul wrote, "Follow my example, as I follow the example of Christ" (1 Corinthians 11:1). Paul, who often wrote using the metaphor of running a race, was describing what we call "baton passing."

Most often, "baton passing" happens between two people who are both living, who communicate personally with ongoing dialogue. The writer of Hebrews recognized another powerful exchange: historical mentoring—looking to role models or "heroes and heroines of the faith" as examples to follow. In Hebrews 11, we have one of the most amazing lists in the Bible. These men and women of faith, both named and unnamed, serve as ongoing illustrations of the benefits of devoting our lives to God and living by faith. These baton-passers are a part of the ongoing "great cloud of witnesses" mentioned in Hebrews 12.

The closing chapter in Hebrews leaves us with these words, "Remember your leaders, who spoke the word of God to you. Consider the outcome of their way of life and imitate their faith" (Hebrews 13:7).

Wrapped up in this verse are three practical applications to the subject of heroes and heroines, role models, and historical mentors.

Introduction

First, we are told, "Remember your leaders." Too often we fail to see ourselves in connection with the rest of humanity throughout all of history. We view today as an isolated moment in time rather than a continuation of God's sovereign plan to reconcile the world to Himself. This isolation keeps us from relating meaningfully to great heroes and heroines of faith who have gone before us and robs us of some of the most powerful role models and mentors we could ever hope to have.

Imagine it! Simply by reading a book, listening to audio, or watching a video, you can learn the secrets of doing great things for God from some of the greatest mentors of the Christian faith. While these faith runners were alive, only a handful of people could get close to them. Regardless of influence and popularity, most people have a fairly small inner network of confidants who spend time with them, share their heart, and participate in their struggles of faith. Resources like this book, however, allow us a window into their life of faith, even when many walked this earth hundreds of years before us. We can read entries from their journals, sit in their meetings, watch their adventures unfold, and observe them in their best, as well as most vulnerable, moments. To do so, we must first remember our leaders.

Second, we are challenged to "consider the outcome of their way of life." Many of the sacrifices on the road to greatness in God's eyes are only brought into perspective when viewed from the end, looking back. Perhaps you've heard the old saying, "Hindsight is 20/20." Often the choices we make in life can only be accurately evaluated when looking back on them. We can see both the consequences of mistakes and the benefits of positive decisions. When we're no longer in the moment, we can gain a clearer perspective on the journey.

A classic illustration of this truth comes from the life of a man named C.T. Studd (his biography appears in chapter 4). Born in the 1800s, C.T. grew up in a wealthy family in England and made a name for himself through playing cricket (a British version of baseball). He later shocked the sports world by answering the call of Hudson Taylor (chapter 15) and sailing for China as a missionary.

While in China, this twenty-five-year-old missionary received final

Introduction

confirmation of the inheritance he knew would be coming from his father's fortune. By today's standards, he was independently wealthy.

In short, C.T. gave his fortune away to the likes of D.L. Moody (chapter 14) and George Müller (chapter 6), who God used to impact millions of people in life and faith. Many in the world might see C.T. as "twice the fool," setting aside a sports career and his wealth for the sake of "missionary work." In hindsight, C.T.'s life impacted more people for Christ than his athleticism or fortune could have ever amassed had he held on to them.

Third, we are urged to "imitate their faith." Notice that we are not exhorted to imitate their lives. We are told to imitate their faith. We are often tempted to imitate the actions of our heroes and heroines. We somehow believe that to be significant we have to become just like them. But God has a race marked out just for us, just for you. It is the faith of others, not necessarily their actions, that is worthy of our imitation.

The people featured in this book are not perfect. This book is about twenty faithful "runners" who not only passed on their faith, but lived it out in a real, vibrant way. They made terrible mistakes, had to learn time and again along the way, and at times, even ran from and doubted God. Sound familiar? That's why their stories are so valuable. They meet us where we are.

If we'll give these flawed yet faithful figures the opportunity, they can serve as our teachers and mentors in loving God and others well as we receive and pass the baton of faith in our generation. So, learn all you can from faithful runners. Above all, don't copy their life, imitate their faith.

It's your turn!

Remember your leaders. Consider the outcome of their way of life. Imitate their faith. These are powerful admonitions. But the real power of these truths rests on the very next verse: "Jesus Christ is the same yesterday and today and forever" (Hebrews 13:8).

You may have heard that verse quoted many times. But rarely is it placed in its original context. Hebrews 13:7-8 make up one complete paragraph and are connected by one common thought. The entire point of verse eight is to emphasize that God wants to continue doing in us the very work He did in the lives of believers who have gone before us. The God we serve today is the same God they served fifty or five hundred or five thousand years ago.

It's important that as you seek to learn from those who have gone before, you keep your eyes fixed on Jesus, "the author and perfecter of our faith" (Hebrews 12:2). Don't get too discouraged by measuring your faith against others. Although their examples can be valuable, ultimately Jesus is the one you must imitate. He "authored" your faith, and He promises to "perfect" it. If you focus on Him, you too, can do valuable things to advance God's Kingdom!

The Kingdom-laboring, baton-passing life is not an easy one. But we are not alone. We are surrounded by a great cloud of witnesses who have modeled this life of faith for us. As you remember them, consider the outcome of their way of life, and imitate their faith, you can write new chapters for future generations who will follow in your footsteps. It's your turn!

Maximize Your Personal & Group Experience:

Take five minutes and read "Getting the Most Out of This Book" and "Group Study Tips." You'll be glad you did!

PART I

IT'S MY TURN TO LIVE WITH A HEART ON FIRE

1

KEITH GREEN (1954-1982)

DECLARATION 1 – IT'S MY TURN TO LOVE GOD WITH PASSION AND INTENTIONALITY

Keith Green had always dreamed of being a successful singer and songwriter. Fame and success, however, took a backseat to Jesus once Keith became a Christian. After finding his way through the maze of values that were so common in the late 1960s and early 70s, Keith poured his life into challenging the Church to move beyond complacent religious activity and to make Jesus their first love and highest priority. His message was fiery, and at times, controversial. Keith's heart, however, radiated an unyielding passion for Jesus, and his music stands today as a testimony to that single-minded love.

Countless people have been touched by the music that Keith wrote out of his ever-deepening relationship with God. One popular chorus, "O Lord, You're Beautiful," came out of one of his intimate times with God. "The Lord brought me right into the throne room, and I sang to Him and just worshipped," Keith said about the song. That passion to know Jesus is reflected in the lyrics:

O Lord, You're beautiful.
　Your face is all I seek.

For when Your eyes are on this child,
Your grace abounds to me...

NOTHING WAS dearer to Keith than knowing God in a deep and abiding way. To Keith, worship meant more than just singing a few songs and offering a prayer or two. "If you praise and worship Jesus with your mouth but your life doesn't praise and worship Him, there's something wrong," he once said.

As Keith grew in his faith, he became consumed with a desire to see others worship God in deeper ways that moved them to worship God with the entirety of their life. He saw that while many people went to church or to Christian concerts, very few of them truly seemed passionate about Jesus. Keith was burdened by the idea of how that must grieve God, and he wanted to do something about it.

One year when he sang at Jesus Northwest, a large Christian music festival, he sensed that the whole event was nothing more than a party. The crowds were enjoying great music, but no one had really challenged them to draw near to God. When it was his turn to take the stage, Keith brought a tough message to the audience. He quoted a passage of Scripture from Amos and told them that God hated their festivals and that what God really wanted was their hearts. Keith urged the people to fall in love with Jesus, and thousands responded.

In 1979, Keith experienced a personal revival, and his fervor swept through the group of people closest to him. His heart broken by Christians living a compromised, lukewarm faith, Keith believed God wanted to take the spirit of revival across the nation. The perfect place to start seemed to be in Tulsa, Oklahoma, his next scheduled concert stop. Keith felt God's calling to offer not just one concert, but a whole week of services on the campus of Oral Roberts University. He received permission to hold three evening programs and began preparing for the work he was sure God wanted to do.

The first two evenings seemed successful, as many people responded to his messages. Keith, however, was discontent. He believed God wanted more for the university. He also believed God was going to move powerfully in Tulsa to bring about a city-wide revival.

The third evening, ORU's Mabee Center was packed with nearly 4,500 people. Keith fasted and prayed all day, listening for the message God wanted him to share.

The service opened with a time of praise and worship. With God's presence filling the auditorium, Keith began sharing a list of sins God had told him were present on the campus. He challenged the audience members to confess their sins. A flood of individuals streamed forward to kneel or lie on their faces before God. As they came, Keith played the piano, not watching to see what was happening, but focusing on the Lord. He tearfully called for God to send His Spirit and break the hearts of everyone present.

Keith opened the microphone to anyone who had something they felt they needed to confess. Many made their way down the packed aisles to the front. Admissions of not supporting the campus staff and breaking curfew led to deeper confessions of drug use and sexual immorality. With each confession came a greater sense of God's presence in that place.

As confessions continued, Keith didn't want to be in the spotlight, nor did he want to interfere with the Holy Spirit's movement. So, Keith crawled under the piano to get on his knees and worship God. He began praising God for His presence and for aligning his heart with what God was bringing about. Keith had correctly heard the Holy Spirit and was obedient.

God brought revival not only to ORU, but to many people, in many places, over the months and years that followed. God used Keith's passionate and surrendered heart on fire to fuel deeper love, worship, and times of intimacy with God for many.

In addition to countless concerts and music albums (which he made available at the cost of "whatever you can afford"), Keith shared his passion with the Body of Christ by speaking and writing through Last Days Ministries, the organization he founded with his wife, Melody. His life-impact was profound and widespread. When he was only twenty-eight, he and two of his children were killed in a plane crash. At his memorial service, Melody said, "I know that Keith is where he wanted to be most. His heart was so with the Lord—he just had such a desire and burning to be close to Jesus. And he really didn't care about this life!"

Keith's passionate life of worship and intimacy with God continues to inspire and challenge people to experience an up-close and intimate relationship with God.

Keith's Significant Contribution
Keith's widespread ministry through writing, teaching, and music challenged Christians everywhere to go beyond spiritual apathy, embracing total surrender to God. He surrendered his talents and gifts to God, eventually using the vehicle of music to challenge his generation to reach the world.

Recommended Reading
No Compromise, by Melody Green

Notable Quote
"One thing I asked God for in that prayer time was His heart. That's the only thing I needed from Him."

IT'S MY TURN TO...

ENGAGE THE STORY

Before reading Keith's story, how would you have defined worship? What do your personal times of worship currently involve?

KEITH SAID, "If you praise and worship Jesus with your mouth and your life does not praise and worship Him, there's something wrong." What does it mean for you to praise and worship God with your life and not just your mouth?

ENGAGE GOD'S WORD

READ Psalms 149:1-5 and 150. Notice the diverse styles of -worship. How could you practice more diversity in your worship of God?

WHAT DO Romans 12:1-2 and Colossians 3:1-17 teach us about what it should look like to worship God with our lives?

ENGAGE MY LIFE

CAREFULLY READ PSALM 139:23-24. Keith often asked God to examine his life. He wanted to avoid the lack of passion for Jesus that he so often saw in Christian circles. Take some time to ask God to expose anything that is keeping you from passionately worshipping God with your life.

KEITH WAS passionate about pointing people back to Jesus. Listen to some of Keith's music. A great place to start is "Keith Green: The Greatest Hits" album. Ask God to meet with you as you worship and reflect on the ways that He has challenged you today.

THE MORE TIME we spend with God, the more passionate our worship will become. Right now, schedule and commit a time to spend alone with God this week—maybe an hour, an afternoon, even a whole day. You can spend the time praying, meditating on scripture, journaling, exercising, listening to worship music, enjoying a snack or meal with God, resting in God's presence, etc.—whatever helps you draw near to God.

FOR FURTHER REFLECTION & ENGAGEMENT

WHAT DID I learn from Keith Green's life and story?

DID Keith's story stir something in me I need to pay attention to and talk to God about?

WHAT CLEAR, MEASURABLE "NEXT STEP" should I take in response to what God is showing me?

WHO IN THE Kingdom community will I ask to encourage me in this and keep me accountable?

WHY THIS LESSON, this day? What's God up to in deepening my faith and multiplying His Kingdom?

2

JOSIAH HENSON (1789-1883)

DECLARATION 2 – IT'S MY TURN TO SACRIFICIALLY LAY DOWN MY LIFE FOR GOD AND OTHERS

Those born into slavery don't spend a lot of time thinking about being famous, they just want to be free. Josiah Henson, however, became both famous and free. He also helped numerous people find freedom through his life of love and sacrifice.

After Harriet Beecher Stowe read his memoirs, Josiah became the inspiration for the main character in her best-selling novel, Uncle Tom's Cabin, a book which President Lincoln credited with helping to lay the groundwork for the Civil War. Like "Uncle Tom," Josiah longed to be free. Once liberated, he willingly risked his own freedom to help others find theirs.

Josiah and his family grew up in Maryland. He came to know Jesus through his mother, who often quoted scripture to him. She sent Josiah to regular house meetings led by John McKenny, a nearby preacher. At one of those gatherings, he heard a sermon on Hebrews 2:9: how "by God's grace, Jesus should taste death for everyone." Josiah, deeply moved by that good news of God's love and sacrifice, committed his life to Jesus.

Soon after, Josiah sensed God's clear calling and mission: to help whomever he could to know and experience God's love and freedom.

Josiah was determined to fulfill his mission regardless of personal cost and sacrifice, a price he willingly paid even for those who enslaved him. Once, when his master got into a drunken brawl, Josiah defended him. His reward? Another white man broke both Josiah's shoulder blades. Josiah often prayed for his masters, burdened that they didn't know the love of Christ. Although they often mistreated him, he declined to run away. He remained loyal and refused to compromise his integrity.

In time, Josiah began preaching. His lack of a formal education didn't deter him. He learned by listening to and studying other great preachers. During a trip between his home in Maryland and his master's brother's plantation in Kentucky, he was ordained in the Methodist Episcopal Church. His preaching opened opportunities to raise funds to buy his freedom. Josiah's life seemed promising.

Hope soon faded, however, when Josiah's life-course was rerouted. His master sold him to a slave owner in the Deep South. That event jolted Josiah. His faith faltered. Feeling God had forsaken him, he decided to kill his traveling companions and escape as they traveled down the river toward his new plantation. As he raised his axe to kill his master's nephew, however, he suddenly realized what he was about to do. "I shrunk back, laid down the axe, and thanked God, as I have done every day since, that I had not committed murder," he wrote in his memoirs. "[I then made] a solemn resolution to resign myself to the will of God, and take with thankfulness, if I could, but with submission, at all events, whatever he might decide should be my lot." And before Josiah could be sold, God intervened. His master's nephew fell sick, and Josiah returned to Kentucky, nursing him back to health.

That event charted a new course for Josiah. He decided to rescue his family from slavery once and for all. They crossed the Ohio River, with Josiah carrying his two young sons over his shoulders in a homemade knapsack. The Henson family nearly starved as they traveled across the Ohio wilderness on foot, and the skin on Josiah's back was completely worn after carrying his sons in a pouch for so long. When they finally arrived at Lake Erie, a ship captain agreed to take them to

Buffalo. From there, they could cross into Canada and possess the freedom they longed for. Josiah was overcome with gratitude at the captain's generosity. When they arrived in Buffalo, he promised the captain, "I'll use my freedom well; I'll give my soul to God."

After forty-one years of slavery, Josiah and his family were free. Freedom, however, came with no provision. Josiah found employment in Fort Erie, where he rented and cleaned out an old pigsty for the family to live. Josiah worked hard. He not only gained his employer's respect but also obtained livestock for his family. "I felt that my toils and sacrifices for freedom had not been in vain," he said. His work and toil in helping life flourish had not been wasted.

In time, Josiah's success drew the attention of other newly-free families. They wanted to know how to buy and establish land for themselves and looked to Josiah for leadership. Josiah helped build a permanent settlement and refuge for former slaves in the town of Dawn, Ontario.

God continued to use Josiah's willing hands, heart, mind, and voice. He became a prominent speaker in the anti-slavery movement. His biography was published in 1849. It inspired many. So much so, that Josiah was invited to travel to Europe, where he met Queen Victoria and spoke ninety-nine times in England and Scotland.

Although grateful for the opportunities, simply talking about abolition was no longer enough for Josiah. "After I had tasted the blessings of freedom, my mind reverted to those whom I knew were groaning in captivity, and I at once proceeded to take measures to free as many as I could," he said. Josiah risked being re-enslaved by returning to the United States to help others find the freedom he enjoyed. His first journey involved a solo trek of walking four-hundred miles in leading a friend's family to freedom.

That was the first of many trips. In all, Josiah helped free 118 slaves through the Underground Railroad. Helping so many people find freedom from the cruel hand of slavery was "one of the greatest sources of my happiness," he said. The gain was well worth the sacrifice.

Josiah Henson continued to travel, preach, and speak out against slavery as he had voice and stamina to do so. He shared with countless others the hope and freedom found in Jesus, who modeled the greatest sacrifice in setting us free.

Josiah's Significant Contribution
After four decades as a slave, Josiah Henson became a well-known writer, preacher, abolitionist, and conductor in the Underground Railroad. He led his family to freedom, then went to great lengths to ensure the freedom and future happiness of more than one hundred other slaves. Josiah demonstrated selfless love for family, friends, and strangers by putting their freedom above his own comfort and safety.

Recommended Reading
The Road to Dawn: Josiah Henson and the Story That Sparked the Civil War, by Jared A. Brock

Notable Quote
"In the course of my preaching I tried to impress upon them the importance of the obligations they were under; first, to God, for their deliverance; and then, secondly, to their fellow-men, to do all that was in their power to bring others out of bondage."

IT'S MY TURN TO ...

ENGAGE THE STORY

Josiah did not allow his background, his lack of education, nor his lack of formal training to deter him from sacrificially laboring for God's Kingdom. Have you ever felt unqualified to make a Kingdom impact in our world? Despite your background or qualifications, how do you think God wants to use you? Will you live sacrificially to carry out His will?

. . .

It's My Turn

WHEN JOSIAH LOST HOPE, he was tempted to take things into his own hands. Thankful that he did not commit murder, he made a vow to trust the will of God, and to submit to "all events, whatever [God] might decide should be [his] lot." Are there areas in your life where you need to submit to the circumstances you are placed in, with thanksgiving, trusting God's plans and timing?

ENGAGE GOD'S WORD

READ MARK 10:45 and Luke 4:14-21. List and reflect on all the things that Jesus was sent to do. What does that mean for those who follow Him?

READ JOHN 15:12-13. In what ways do you see that Josiah had become like Jesus in laying down his life to love others. What could this practically look like in your life?

ENGAGE MY LIFE

JOSIAH'S LIFE was devoted to proclaiming the good news of Jesus Christ, sacrificing his own life to enable the freedom of others, and humbly persevering in the face of difficulty. Would you say that any of these Kingdom values are evident in your own life? Talk to God about how you might need to cultivate these.

JOSIAH PUT the freedom of others above his own comfort and safety, counting the gain well worth the sacrifice. What is God asking you to sacrifice in "laying down your life" for others: money, time, comfort, freedom, your very life? Ask God. Be willing to do whatever He prompts you to do.

FOR FURTHER REFLECTION & ENGAGEMENT

WHAT DID I learn from Josiah Henson's life and story?

DID Josiah's story stir something in me I need to pay attention to and talk to God about?

WHAT CLEAR, MEASURABLE "NEXT STEP" should I take in response to what God is showing me?

WHO IN THE Kingdom community will I ask to encourage me in this and keep me accountable?

WHY THIS LESSON, this day? What's God up to in deepening my faith and multiplying His Kingdom?

3

FLORENCE NIGHTINGALE (1820-1910)

DECLARATION 3 – IT'S MY TURN TO LOVE AND SERVE WITH HUMILITY

Overlooking the plight of the sick and poor would have been easy for an upper-class girl like Florence Nightingale; the attractive, popular, and pampered daughter of a prominent English banker. Her sheltered life was filled with social events and mindless activities where most in her social class paid no attention to the suffering around them. But Florence was paying attention and could no longer ignore those who didn't have access to the privileges she possessed. At seventeen, her heart was stirred. At twenty-two, her calling found clarity: she was to devote her life to God by entering the profession of nursing.

Nursing in the mid-1800s was far from a respectable move. In fact, her family was horrified at her announcement and "forbade" her to pursue it. Nurses were often seen as careless, dirty, immoral drunkards. Working conditions were horrible, hospitals unsanitary, and the nursing system was chaotic and largely ineffective.

Despite the challenges, Florence formally began her nursing career at thirty-one. Fulfilling her calling was well worth the cost. She continued to learn all she could about nursing and hospital administration. Her desire was to help transform the profession.

In 1853, Florence became Superintendent of London's Institution for the Care of Sick Gentlewomen in Distressed Circumstances. The vast improvements she made administratively and her dedicated caregiving as a nurse earned great admiration from patients, the public, and the poor alike.

Florence's passion met opportunity. She was asked to become the superintendent of nurses at Kings College Hospital. As she was making plans to accept the invitation, an item in the London Times about the Crimean War caught her attention. "...no sufficient preparations have been made for the proper care of the wounded. Not only are there no dressers and nurses... Men (are) kept in some cases for a week without the hand of a medical man..." The article ended with the challenge, "Are there no devoted women amongst us able...to go forth to minister to the sick and suffering soldiers? ... Are none... ready for such a work of mercy?" Florence's heart was stirred. Her longtime friend Sidney Herbert, the Secretary of War, asked her to pull together a group of nurses and head to the Crimean Peninsula immediately.

Florence gathered nearly forty nurses and responded to the call. Upon arrival, they discovered horrible conditions. A makeshift hospital had been set up in a dirty, rundown barracks with no kitchen, beds, linens, cups, chairs, or operating tables. A line of wounded soldiers stretching four miles awaited treatment. Rats, maggots, and fleas were everywhere. The roof leaked. The place was void of lamplight and running water. More soldiers died from contracted disease and infection than from battle wounds. Adding to the chaos, the hospital was completely disorganized and inefficient, and Florence faced opposition from stubborn administrators who resented her expertise.

Florence didn't flinch. She got to work immediately to develop a system for nursing the wounded while simultaneously formulating plans to secure beds, bandages, cleaning supplies, clothing, eating utensils, and proper ventilation for the hospital. Often, she used her own money or solicited donations from friends in England to purchase needed supplies. Within weeks, amazing differences could be seen in

It's My Turn

the sanitary conditions of the hospital and the morale and health of the wounded.

Amid all the reform and administration, Florence's first commitment was still to the patients she served. "Christ is the author of our profession," she said. She wanted to care for the sick and give them hope in the same manner as Jesus had done. Florence spent hours in the wards looking after patients. Often, she could be found at the beds of the most severe cases. Florence nursed many deemed "hopeless" back to health and saved limbs scheduled for amputation.

The patients saw her as an angel. The London Times reported, "When all the medical officers have retired for the night and silence and darkness have settled down upon those miles of prostrate sick, she may be observed alone, with a little lamp in her hand, making her solitary rounds." She became known as "The lady with the lamp."

Florence Nightingale rose to a position of respect and authority because of her resourcefulness, calm and caring spirit, and her ability to make significant changes in the nursing system. So significant were her contributions to the medical field, she was later deemed "the mother of the modern nursing profession." Still, Florence resisted all the accolades and recognition that came her way.

When the war ended, Florence stayed at the hospital a few months longer to care for the remaining wounded. She wanted them to return home safely and whole as well. A British war ship was provided for her return, and all of England prepared to celebrate her arrival with brass bands and ceremonies.

Florence had other plans. She quietly booked passage on a small steamer for the trip to England. Once on British soil, she traveled by train as an unknown passenger, walked home from the train station, and entered her home unannounced, through the back door. The only affirming fanfare important to Florence was "well done" given by God.

Florence's Significant Contribution
Florence Nightingale used the unique mind and skills God gave her to transform the nursing profession into a respectable field. She wrote,

Notes on Nursing, a valuable resource and guide to the profession. Her care to the sick and poor, her innovative reform of the nursing system, and her written resources earned her the title, "The Mother of Modern Nursing."

Recommended Reading
A Lost Commander, Florence Nightingale, by Mary Raymond Shipman Andrews

Notable Quote
"Oh, Lord, thou puttest into my heart this great desire to devote myself to the sick and sorrowful. I offer it to thee."

IT'S MY TURN TO ...

ENGAGE THE STORY

FLORENCE WAS COMPELLED to enter a profession her family (and many others) didn't approve of at the time. How would you have responded to family and friends knowing that God's calling for your life wasn't approved of or valued by others?

FLORENCE SET ASIDE A COMFORTABLE, profitable, esteemed position at King's College Hospital to care for the wounded and dying in the Crimean War. What life plans would you have difficulty abandoning if God nudged you in another direction?

ENGAGE GOD'S WORD

READ PHILIPPIANS 2:1-11. What characteristics does Paul tell us mark a life of humility? Can you think of specific examples where

Jesus displayed humility? How are these characteristics thriving or lacking in your life?

READ MATTHEW 25:34-40. How should these verses shape the way that we see and serve others?

ENGAGE MY LIFE

GOD PLACED a clear desire in Florence's heart to devote her life to care for the sick. What desires has God placed in your heart to actively serve others? If you are not sure, take some time now to ask Him to give you a heart for the people He desires you to serve.

FLORENCE CAME HOME SECRETLY to avoid praise and recognition. List some ways you can practice humility this week by serving or benefitting someone anonymously. Have fun with it! Do it cheerfully for the sake of love and to the praise and honor of God alone.

FOR FURTHER REFLECTION & ENGAGEMENT

WHAT DID I learn from Florence Nightingale's life and story?

DID Florence's story stir something in me I need to pay attention to and talk to God about?

WHAT CLEAR, MEASURABLE "NEXT STEP" should I take in response to what God is showing me?

. . .

Who in the Kingdom community will I ask to encourage me in this and keep me accountable?

Why this lesson, this day? What's God up to in deepening my faith and multiplying His Kingdom?

4

C.T. STUDD (1862-1931)

DECLARATION 4 – IT'S MY TURN TO SAY YES TO GOD WITH RECKLESS ABANDON

At fifty years of age, C.T. (Charles Thomas) Studd was not the prime candidate for a frontier missions thrust to the heart of unevangelized Africa. At least not from a human point of view. He had already served in China and India, helping lead the Cambridge Seven (a group of English university students who committed to go to China after hearing D.L. Moody preach) overseas in 1885 with China Inland Mission. He also toured American universities in the early stages of the Student Volunteer Movement, which mobilized more than twenty thousand college students as career missionaries! And, C.T.'s health had been failing for fifteen years. His severe asthma alone was reason enough to keep him out of tropical Africa.

But in Liverpool, England, in 1908, C.T. noticed a sign that appealed to his curiosity and sense of humor. "Cannibals want missionaries," the sign proclaimed. Why, sure they do, for more reasons than one, C.T. thought. He was hooked. He had to go in and hear more.

Inside, Dr. Karl Krumm was telling of his experiences walking across Africa. Dr. Krumm explained that in the middle of the continent lived countless tribes who had never heard the story of Jesus Christ. Explorers, big-game hunters, traders, European officials, and scientists had all been to those regions. But as for Christians? None had ever gone to tell about Jesus.

Humiliation sank deep into C.T.'s soul. "Why have no Christians gone?" he wondered. God replied, "Why don't you go?" "The doctors won't permit it," C.T. rebutted. As in the story of Job, God doubled down: "Am I not the Good Physician? Can I not take you through? Can I not keep you there?" C.T. had no excuses. The call was clear. He was going to Africa.

C.T. needed a plan. After all, he was in ill health and already beyond the prime of his life. He discussed a strategy with Dr. Krumm, and the two of them planned an exploratory journey to southern Sudan, a thousand miles south of Khartoum. The rapid spread of Islam in that area gave them both a sense of urgency to plant a chain of mission stations. They wanted to share the gospel of Jesus Christ with the people as quickly as possible.

C.T.'s next major need was for funding. He had long since given away any wealth he possessed, and he had no money left to go to Africa. He outlined the challenge to a group of businessmen. They responded to God's stirring and committed to back the project. However, they presented one important qualifier: C.T. must see a doctor and be given medical clearance.

The doctor examined C.T. and reported this conclusion: C.T. would die if he ventured south of Khartoum. He must agree to the donors' precondition or there would be no funds. C.T. could never comply with this kind of limitation. It would undermine the entire project. He responded to the group of businessmen with these words, "Gentlemen, God has called me to go, and I will go. I will blaze the trail, though my grave may only become a stepping-stone that younger men may follow."

It seemed crazy—a penniless, fifty-year-old man with asthma and malaria, bent on going to the heart of Africa. But C.T. had learned that God laughs at impossibilities. His years of service under the leadership of Hudson Taylor and the China Inland Mission had taught him that in the crucible of life, God could be trusted. He would proceed by faith.

Sure enough, God provided the supplies, and C.T. went on the exploratory mission. While in Sudan, he heard about masses of people in the Belgian Congo who had never heard of Christ. That settled it. C.T. could never spend the remainder of his years in England when Africans had such a desperate need for the gospel.

With the exploratory mission completed, C.T. returned to England aflame with a vision for this New Crusade. He traveled to Cambridge and gave an impassioned plea on behalf of the unreached peoples in the heart of Africa. Fueling the fires of his cause were two booklets: The Shame of Christ and The Chocolate Soldier.

Before long, C.T. returned to Africa. The night before he left, he spoke with a young man who questioned his plans. "Is it a fact that at fifty-two, you mean to leave your country, your home, your wife, and your children?" C.T. responded, "If Jesus Christ be God and died for me, then no sacrifice can be too great for me to make for Him." His words became the motto of the crusade.

C.T. Studd did die in Africa as the doctor predicted—only it was twenty years later! Through his faith and obedience in the face of great sacrifice, many thousands were brought into the Kingdom, and a new mission agency, Worldwide Evangelization Crusade International, was born. His last written words were, "Let God be magnified! Hallelujah!"

C.T.'s Significant Contribution
One of the fruits of C.T. Studd's radical obedience was the formation of the Heart of Africa Mission. Later known as WEC International, the Heart of Africa Mission was a new agency birthed out of his pioneer ministry among the unreached peoples of central Africa. Not only did C.T. answer God's call, he also mobilized others to radically obey God, challenging thousands to join him on the front lines of the battle for the spread of the gospel.

Recommended Reading
C.T. Studd, Cricketer and Pioneer, by Norman Grubb

Notable Quote
"Some wish to live within the sound of church or chapel bell, I want to run a rescue shop within a yard of hell."

IT'S MY TURN TO …

ENGAGE THE STORY

Describe what your dream career or "perfect retirement" would look like? C.T. gave up a well-paying cricket career at age 24 as well as his potential for retirement at age 50. How does C.T.'s obedience challenge the way you might view your personal life plans?

C.T. HAD many obstacles that might have kept him from serving the Lord: health issues, age, lack of money, etc. What obstacles in your life could potentially exclude you from serving God's Kingdom? Do you believe God can use you and those hurdles to bring glory to His name?

ENGAGE GOD'S WORD

READ MATTHEW 4:18-22 What are some of the things these men walked away from when answering Jesus' call to follow Him? Notice how they responded to Jesus. Their obedience was immediate and didn't require an explanation. How does their example of reckless abandon challenge you in following Jesus?

READ MATTHEW 19:16-28. C.T. was serving as a missionary in China when he received news his father left him a very large inheritance. C.T. had just finished reading, "If you want to be perfect, go, sell your possessions and give to the poor, and you will have treasure in heaven. Then come, follow me" (verse 21). C.T. immediately decided to do likewise, giving his inheritance to other kingdom laborers (His gifts were instrumental in the establishment of D.L. Moody's Bible College, George Müller's ministry to orphans, and the Salvation Army). What made C.T. different than the rich young man in the story? Does your life more resemble C.T. or the rich young man? How so?

ENGAGE MY LIFE

When asked about his choice to leave everything behind, C.T. declared, "If Jesus Christ be God and died for me, then no sacrifice can be too great for me to make for him." In what areas of your life have you recently said "yes" to God with reckless abandon?

C.T. said, "How could I spend the best years of my life in living for the honors of this world when thousands of souls are perishing every day?" Ask God to burden your heart, give you courage, and help you sacrifice whatever is necessary to reach those who are spiritually lost.

FOR FURTHER REFLECTION & ENGAGEMENT

What did I learn from C.T. Studd's life and story?

Did C.T.'s story stir something in me I need to pay attention to and talk to God about?

What clear, measurable "next step" should I take in response to what God is showing me?

. . .

Who in the Kingdom community will I ask to encourage me in this and keep me accountable?

Why this lesson, this day? What's God up to in deepening my faith and multiplying His Kingdom?

5

LUIS PALAU (1934–)

DECLARATION 5 – IT'S MY TURN TO TRUST JESUS FOR A GOD-SIZED VISION

If life is a plane ride, Luis Palau Jr. hit severe turbulence just after takeoff. Born in Buenos Aires, Argentina in 1934, Luis was the oldest of five younger sisters and one stepbrother. His father, a construction executive, contracted pneumonia and died when Luis was ten. Luis, away at boarding school, couldn't make it home in time to tell his father goodbye. Luis' family, once affluent, became financially destitute through money mismanagement by former business associates. Luis was forced to leave his education at a British-run boarding school and turn to an entry-level bank job to support the family. The years of working through hardships and providing for his family at a very young age led him to write later in life: "When you face the perils of weariness, carelessness, and confusion, don't pray for an easier life. Pray instead to be a stronger man or woman of God."

Both Luis's parents were believers and influenced his life of faith. In particular, the time Luis spent with his father, though brief, created indelible marks and spiritual deposits of the Christ-following life. At age twelve, Luis committed his life to Christ at a summer camp.

One evening, while Luis was still a teenager, he heard an evangelist from the United States preaching on the radio. He spoke with such passion and conviction about Jesus Christ. The voice over the airwaves was Billy Graham. God sparked something in Luis that day: a vision of the plan and purpose of his life to share the good news of the gospel to millions around the world. Luis said in that moment, "I knew it was my time."

Luis began preaching on the streets and sharing on the radio. His offering seemed small for a God-sized vision. Regardless, Luis remained faithful. One day, a faith-filled pastor from California, Ray Stedman, heard Luis preaching and asked to speak with him. Ray affirmed what God was doing and asked Luis if he ever considered seminary. Ray explained that his church helped people called to missions come to the U.S. and study and train. Luis said he didn't think that would ever be possible financially. But God had a plan.

Luis, now twenty-six, moved to Portland, Oregon to attend a graduate program at Multnomah Bible College. Life moved quickly once there. Luis met and married his wife and partner in life and ministry, Patricia. He graduated from the program, became a U.S. citizen, and he and Pat spent the next eight years as missionaries to Mexico and Columbia.

Not long before Luis and Pat left Oregon to serve as missionaries, they had another profound encounter with Billy Graham. This time, in person. Luis was asked to be a translator for Billy Graham at a nearby Crusade. That experience added fuel to the vision God had placed in Luis's heart.

In Columbia, Luis and Pat served faithfully in their assigned task: preach and plant churches. Luis worked faithfully, but his heart was restless. The vision of preaching in mass gatherings for the transformation of the world wouldn't leave him. In 1966, the vision began to have visible recognition. The opportunity came to launch a crusade and preach in Bogota, Columbia. The task was daunting and the obstacles many. The least of which was a political and sometimes violent revolution taking place in Columbia. Luis and his team trusted God in the challenge. They decided to invite as many churches to be involved as possible, regardless of denomination. Churches were to pray, invite guests, and join a unified parade to march down the city streets of Bogota to a central gathering place where the gospel would

It's My Turn

be shared. Over 20,000 people gathered that day. The movement of God was powerful, and many responded by receiving Christ as Lord.

Columbia was the first of many crusades to come. In 1970, the Billy Graham organization invested $100,000 into helping Luis launch his own evangelism outreach to share the good news. The vision God gave to Luis as a faithful young boy began bearing enormous Kingdom fruit. Luis Palau and the Palau Association have shared the good news of Jesus Christ for sixty-plus years now to over a billion people in over seventy countries, including major crusades in such cities as London, Hong Kong, Singapore, Chicago, Moscow, Madrid, Mexico City, Buenos Aires, New York, and Washington D.C.

In addition to his speaking ministry, Luis's radio ministry has reached more than 5,800 outlets in over fifty countries, and his Spanish Bible institute has enrolled over 44,000 students. Through all the Kingdom success, Luis kept his focus on God.

In 1980, Pat was diagnosed with cancer. The Palau's commitment didn't waiver. They promised to serve the Lord and work toward the vision He had given them for as long as they both had breath. Miraculously, Pat was healed.

In January 2018, Luis announced that he had incurable lung cancer. His prognosis was only a few months to several months at best. Now, two and a half years later at the time of this writing, Luis continues to speak on the radio, write, and share good news however he's able. After all, as Luis says, "Evangelism is not an option for the Christian life."

"Only God can change people," Luis once said. That's why when movie producers asked Luis if they could make a movie about his tremendous life of Kingdom impact that began as a small boy and a seed-sized vision, Luis said, "Only if it's about Him, not about me. It has to be about what God has done."

Luis's Significant Contribution
Luis Palau has delivered the good news of Jesus to millions worldwide through crusades, radio broadcasts, and written publications. Luis continues to teach and demonstrate to laboring Christ-followers what

God can do when we trust Him to accomplish a vision far beyond ourselves regardless of obstacles and circumstances.

Recommended Reading and Viewing
Palau: A Life on Fire, by Luis Palau and Paul J. Pastor

Where is God When Bad Things Happen: Finding Solace in Times of Trouble, by Luis Palau

Palau (the film), palauthemovie.com

Notable Quote
"One encounter with Jesus Christ is enough to change you, instantly, forever."

IT'S MY TURN TO …

ENGAGE THE STORY

Luis was only a teenager when God gave him a vision of one day sharing the gospel with millions. Despite the odds being stacked against him, (his age, lack of funds, limited training) Luis immediately obeyed the call and began preaching in the streets. What obstacles are you allowing to hinder you from seeing and/or obeying God's plans for your life?

EVEN THOUGH GOD gave Luis a vision as a teenager, it took many years to see it come to fulfillment. Can you think of specific examples in this story, that would have encouraged Luis to continue on? Where do you see God's hand at work?

ENGAGE GOD'S WORD

It's My Turn

READ ROMANS 4:18-22 God gave Abraham a seemingly impossible vision. How did Abraham respond to the Lord? Abraham is not known for doing anything extravagant, but simply taking God at His word and arranging his life around God's vision. Ask God to help you believe him for the plans and purposes he has for your life.

READ MATTHEW 9:35-38. Imagine yourself walking with Jesus and seeing the crowds. Now, imagine walking with Luis while he looked over crowds at evangelistic events. Finally, imagine looking out at all the lost people in your everyday life. What does this passage tell us the world needs most? Who has Jesus called to be Kingdom laborers? How can you better live as a Kingdom Laborer, fulfilling the heart of Jesus?

ENGAGE MY LIFE

THINK through the timeline of your life. Write down significant turning points (highs and lows). Spend some time considering how God has used those events to shape you, mature you and employ you as a Kingdom laborer, and write that down at each point.

LUIS HAD a clear vision of what God desired for him, because he spent intimate time with God in constant prayer. This vision was seemingly impossible, but like Abraham, Luis trusted God. Make time this week to dream with God. Ask Him to give you clarity on His vision and purposes for your life. As you pray and ask the Lord to give you vision, begin to write down whatever He shows you.

FOR FURTHER REFLECTION & ENGAGEMENT

WHAT DID I learn from Luis Palau's life and story?

. . .

Did Luis's story stir something in me I need to pay attention to and talk to God about?

What clear, measurable "next step" should I take in response to what God is showing me?

Who in the Kingdom community will I ask to encourage me in this and keep me accountable?

Why this lesson, this day? What's God up to in deepening my faith and multiplying His Kingdom?

6

GEORGE MÜLLER (1805-1898)

DECLARATION 6 – IT'S MY TURN TO LIVE BY RADICAL FAITH

When he was younger, none would have believed that George Müller would become a great man of faith working with orphans in England. George was religious socially, but internally, he denied God was authentic and worth following. In fact, Müller became widely known for his thievery and drunkenness, even stealing from his own father. That all changed, however, when a friend invited George to a college worship gathering where the prayers and message were powerful and sincere. George asked God to make his faith genuine. God did. That encounter lit a fire of bold faith in George that has inspired and challenged many ever since.

George felt called to be a missionary. When his father opposed the idea, George decided not to accept any more money from him. Instead, George committed to trust God to meet his needs. Once, when George needed money for daily provisions, he asked God to help. One hour later, a professor offered him a tutoring job that would pay four times the normal rate! When he couldn't afford his rent, he was offered a free room at a nearby orphanage. These experiences and many like them bolstered his faith in a trustworthy God.

George's next faith step led him to a pastoral position in London. When it became evident that his clergy income came from renting church pews for worship services, he could no longer accept those resources with integrity. He committed to trust God alone to supply his needs. And God provided. Always. George and his family kept only what they needed, never borrowed, and blessed others with any extra they received.

In 1832, George moved to Bristol and began a Breakfast Club for underserved children. He invited children to his house to share a meal and the Scriptures with them. He trusted God to provide whatever was needed. God did. Soon, forty children attended every morning. Still, George felt God wanted to do more. Opportunity came. God called George to start an orphanage.

Though many discouraged the idea and said it wouldn't work, George found a house to rent and scheduled the opening of his first orphanage in 1836. Soon, it was home to twenty-six girls. Forty-two more girls were on a waiting list. Hating to turn any children away, he rented two more houses down the street, and George and his staff began caring for eighty-one children.

George was a visionary who did not know how to think small. When he saw God's vision of caring for and ministering to orphans in Great Britain, he was determined to do it right. He prayed long hours. He fasted. He began to share his burden and vision with others who could partner with him in some way. The undertaking was enormous, but George concluded, "The greatness of the sum required affords me a kind of secret joy; for the greater the difficulty to be overcome, the more will it be seen to the glory of God how much can be done by prayer and faith."

George's faith was realized. God provided. Buildings grew. Some were built, others were bought. Eventually, whole city blocks were owned by Müller's Orphanage which housed, fed, and taught homeless children. It was a tribute to God and what faith can do.

George's faith was vital in his ministry to the orphans as he trusted God to meet the children's daily needs. One morning, over three hundred kids came to breakfast. The table was set, but there was no food. Nevertheless, George gave thanks for what God was going to give them to eat and told the children to sit down. He didn't know where their food would come from, but he knew that somehow, God would provide.

Just then, a baker knocked at the door. He explained that the night before, he hadn't been able to sleep. So, at two o'clock in the morning, he got up and made three batches of bread for the orphanage. A few moments later, a milkman knocked at the door. He had broken a wheel on his cart, and he needed to lighten his load. So, he offered the orphanage ten full cans of free milk! George wrote in his journal, "The Lord not only gives as much as is absolutely necessary for His work, but He gives abundantly."

In his later years, George began preaching around the world. On one trip, the ship ran into thick fog just off the coast of Newfoundland. George needed to be in Quebec by Saturday afternoon to make his first speaking engagement. The captain, however, said the trip was impossible.

"If you cannot find a way to get me there on time, I'll have to ask God to do it," George responded. "I have not missed a single engagement in fifty-two years, and I don't intend to start now. Come down to my cabin with me, and we will pray together." The captain said, "What's the point of praying? The fog is so thick I cannot see to the stern. Look for yourself, Mr. Müller." George simply replied, "I don't need to look. My eye is not on the weather but on the One who controls the weather!"

George began to pray: "Dear God, I come to You now to ask You to do the impossible. You know that I need to be in Quebec by Saturday and that the fog has hemmed us in. Please lift the fog so that the ship can go forward and I will be on time."

George then turned to the captain. "I have known my Lord for fifty-two years, and in all that time I cannot recall a single instance where he has not answered my prayers. I can assure you, the fog has lifted." Sure enough, the fog was completely gone! And by the time the ship docked, the captain had placed his faith in the God whom George trusted so completely.

By 1870, George Müller was operating five orphanages and caring for more than two thousand children! With it all, George knew who deserved the credit. "When it is the Lord's pleasure to remove this servant from my post, people will see that it is I who was dependent on Him and not He who was dependent on me," George said. "He can and will easily raise up another servant, and...the orphan houses will continue to flourish."

George's Significant Contribution
Because of his work in caring for ten thousand orphans, George Müller has been called "The Father of Homeless Waifs." His work continues today through the Müller Foundation, which cares for orphans, provides for the elderly, and contributes to the work of missionaries worldwide. George's lived-out belief that "with God, no emergency is unseen, and no want is unprovided for" became a model for Christians to follow.

Recommended Reading
George Müller, by Faith Coxe Bailey

Notable Quote
"The greater the difficulty overcome, the more will it be seen to the glory of God how much can be done by prayer and faith."

IT'S MY TURN TO ...

ENGAGE THE STORY

When George's trip was delayed because of the weather, the captain focused on the fog before them. What did George choose to keep his focus on? Take note that radical faith always comes from trusting in "the One who controls the weather." Is there a time you have seen this kind of radical faith in your life or someone else's life?

GEORGE STRUGGLED to trust God for the provisions necessary to open an orphanage until he meditated upon Psalm 81:10, "Open your mouth wide and I will fill it." Can you name an area in your life where you feel uncertain that God can or will provide exactly what is needed?

ENGAGE GOD'S WORD

READ MATTHEW 6:25-34. Three times in this passage we are commanded to "not be anxious." When George had no food for the children, he didn't sit and fret, nor did he try to solve the problem. He boldly thanked God in advance for the way He would provide. What areas of your life are creating anxiety that you need to lay at your father's feet today?

GEORGE BELIEVED in the promises of the loving father that we see in Matthew 6:33, and he stayed in alignment with God's plans by "seeking his kingdom first." Read Hebrews 11:6. What does God expect us to believe about Him?

ENGAGE MY LIFE

GEORGE DIDN'T JUST WAKE up one day with some miracle gift of faith. God grew and increased George's faith as George trusted God, one step of faith at a time. What will your next step of faith be? What will you choose to have faith and trust God with today? Ask God what your next faith step should be. Then trust Him to come through!

GEORGE'S radical faith soared on the wings of prayer. Do you spend more time trying to fix things yourself or in conversation with the Father? Commit time this week to continue to talk to God about your faith steps that He brought to mind today.

FOR FURTHER REFLECTION & ENGAGEMENT

What did I learn from George Müller's life and story?

Did George's story stir something in me I need to pay attention to and talk to God about?

What clear, measurable "next step" should I take in response to what God is showing me?

Who in my Kingdom community will I ask to encourage and keep me accountable in this?

Why this lesson, this day? What's God up to in deepening my faith and multiplying His Kingdom?

7

WATCHMAN NEE (1903-1972)

DECLARATION 7 – IT'S MY TURN TO WILLINGLY SUFFER FOR THE KINGDOM OF GOD

Known throughout his school years as an exceptional student, Watchman Nee had plenty of big dreams for future success. Although bright and talented, Watchman could never calculate just how much Kingdom impact his life would bring when he committed his life to Christ. God used Watchman's astute leadership skills to empower the Church in China to grow rapidly. God also allowed Watchman to endure great suffering. In it all, Watchman increasingly learned to trust and depend on the faithfulness of God.

Nee Shu-tsu (Watchman's given name at birth) had heard the gospel since he was a small boy. He learned a lot about God in those years, but he was seventeen when he realized that knowing God meant also serving Him.

"At that time, I was afraid of being saved; for I knew that once I was saved, I must serve the Lord," he said. "...It was impossible for me to set aside the Lord's calling and to desire only salvation." Nee Shu-tsu couldn't simply receive Jesus as his Savior; he knew that Jesus must also be his Lord. That night, he surrendered his life to Jesus as Savior and Lord. God honored his commitment and immediately called Nee Shu-tsu to become a preacher.

The Chinese have a custom of choosing a new name after a significant milestone in life. So, after his conversion, Nee Shu-tsu selected the name Nee To-sheng, in English, "Watchman Nee." He saw himself as the watchman who would sound the warning and deliver the gospel to the people of China.

While attending Trinity College, Watchman began to share his faith with his classmates and hold prayer meetings with new believers. The gospel quickly spread beyond the college campus. Revival came to the city of Foochow. Countless young people came to Christ, and they began to share the gospel to nearby cities and villages. Watchman began to see a vision for churches to be planted throughout China.

As with most God-sized visions, Watchman's endeavor was costly. He faced poverty, sickness, local church and denominational opposition, as well as governmental persecution. Though constantly under attack, he submitted himself to God. He knew God would be faithful and present through it all. Like the apostle Paul, he saw his suffering as a "thorn in the flesh." He also viewed suffering as a way to grow. "You must allow God to give you time to suffer beyond measure," he said, so that "your capacity will be enlarged."

God honored Watchman's faithfulness and used suffering to expand his influence. When Watchman contracted tuberculosis, for example, he had to stop traveling and preaching for a season. Instead of speaking, God put him to writing. Watchman's writings became a valuable tool in God's hands in helping countless believers grow.

Watchman relocated his ministry to Shanghai and worked to build local churches. His ministry flourished. With it, his suffering increased. Watchman suffered at the hands of false witnesses who spread rumors about him and tried to discredit his ministry. His wife's aunt, who disapproved of their marriage, spread evil stories about him. False rumors led a group of co-laboring friends from England to discredit and reject him. Still, with every false story, rejection, and persecution, Watchman refused to defend himself. He stood firm in the Lord, believing God and His truth would prevail.

Suffering, a cup most would prefer to let pass, often yields Kingdom fruit. Watchman endured suffering, and God's Kingdom

It's My Turn

thrived because of it. The Church in Shanghai grew rapidly. With God and momentum on their side, Watchman developed a strategic plan for Shanghai families to move to different areas throughout China, plant churches, and share the gospel. The churches executed the plan. God blessed it, and His Kingdom continued to spread.

In time, however, the Communist Party took note of Watchman's growing ministry. Because of the danger, co-laboring friends urged him to remain in Hong Kong rather than return to mainland China. He responded, "If a mother discovered that her house was on fire, and she herself was outside the house doing the laundry, what would she do? Although she realized the danger, would she not rush into the house? Although I know that my return is fraught with dangers, I know that many brothers and sisters are still inside. How can I not return?"

Soon, the Communist army entered Shanghai and closed all churches. In the spring of 1952, they arrested Watchman. They condemned his faith in Jesus and took exception to his leadership of churches that were not under Communist authority. A 2,296-page indictment against him contained all sorts of false accusations, ranging from espionage and counterrevolutionary activities to immorality and financial mishandlings. He appeared before his accusers twelve straight days. Their verdict? Guilty. Watchman was sentenced to prison at age fifty, and he would never be free again.

Though some details are clear, no one knows the full extent of suffering Watchman endured over the next twenty years. He wasn't allowed contact or communication with the outside world. They confiscated his Bible. His days consisted of eight hours of hard labor. His nights eight hours alone in a dark cell. The remaining eight hours of the day promised long interrogations and brainwashing lectures for "re-education" purposes. The Communists wanted to break him. But Watchman stayed strong. He passed the time by reciting scripture and singing songs he wrote from Bible verses. He shared about Jesus with those around him, and one of the prison guards even became a Christian. Beyond the prison walls, his writings inspired a revival among Chinese students.

Watchman died in confinement in a prison cell on May 30, 1972. Under his pillow, he left a piece of paper on which he had written, "Christ is the Son of God who died for the redemption of sinners and resurrected after three days. This is the greatest truth in the universe. I die because of my belief in Christ. Watchman Nee."

To the very end, Watchman Nee shared the good news he spent his life proclaiming.

Watchman's Significant Contribution
Watchman Nee used preaching, teaching, traveling, correspondence with people, conferences, training, and writing to spread the gospel. His suffering fueled the growth of the Chinese church. Today, there are more than 2,300 churches worldwide, and innumerably more influenced through them because of Watchman's faithful witness for Christ.

Recommended Reading
The Normal Christian Life, by Watchman Nee

Notable Quote
"Lord, I am willing to break my heart that I might satisfy Thy heart."

IT'S MY TURN TO ...

ENGAGE THE STORY

Watchman said, "If you cannot stand the trials of the cross, you cannot become a useful instrument." How can difficulties and trials make you a more useful instrument and "enlarge your capacity," as Watchman said they did for him? (James 1:2-4)

MANY TIMES, Watchman was falsely accused of evil and his enemies spread rumors about him. Yet he never tried to defend himself. Have you ever been falsely accused or been the subject of rumors? How did you respond? Look at Matthew 26:57-64 to see how Jesus responded, which informs us what a godly response to accusation might look like.

ENGAGE GOD'S WORD

READ 1 PETER 4:12-16. What should our response be during times of trials and difficulty? How do you want be able respond to the next difficulty you face? What can you practically do to make that a reality?

READ ACTS 16:22-34. Much like the disciples, Watchman spent time in prison openly praising and praying. What kind of kingdom impact did Watchman and the disciples both have from prison? What if God used your response to trials and suffering to further advance His Kingdom?

ENGAGE MY LIFE

WHENEVER YOU ARE ON MISSION, expect opposition. But when you encounter opposition, look for Kingdom opportunity, just as Watchman did. How much are you willing to endure for the sake of Christ and His Kingdom: Discomfort? Mockery? Economic pain? Loss of relationships? Threats? Torture? Martyrdom? Have a serious conversation with God about what you are willing to live for... and die for.

READ about Christians being persecuted today: Search "Persecuted Christians" online (a great place to start is the Voice of the Martyrs at www.persecution.com). Consider writing a letter to an imprisoned believer and committing to pray for our suffering brothers and sisters around the world.

FOR FURTHER REFLECTION & ENGAGEMENT

What did I learn from Watchman Nee's life and story?

Did Watchman's story stir something in me I need to pay attention to and talk to God about?

What clear, measurable "next step" should I take in response to what God is showing me?

Who in the Kingdom community will I ask to encourage me in this and keep me accountable?

Why this lesson, this day? What's God up to in deepening my faith and multiplying His Kingdom?

8

AMY CARMICHAEL (1867-1951)

DECLARATION 8 – IT'S MY TURN TO DIE TO SELF IN ORDER TO EXALT CHRIST

Amy Carmichael was a fun-loving young girl with an eye for beauty. As she matured in her faith, she began to realize that ultimate beauty came from following Jesus and dying to self. Her love for the Lord led her to India, where she loved and served countless children and fellow workers. As a God-assigned mother and mentor to many, she constantly put her own desires aside so that God's greater beauty and purposes could take center stage.

Amy first learned about dying to self at age seventeen when she and her brothers were on their way home from church in Belfast, Ireland. They came across an elderly woman of little means carrying a heavy bundle. It seemed only right for them to take the bundle and help the woman along. As they did, however, they began noticing the "respectable people" of the community were staring at them. Amy felt ashamed to be publicly associated with someone her culture deemed "undesirable." She was embarrassed and noted how horrible the experience was for her and her brothers.

The elderly woman wasn't the only encounter Amy experienced on her trudge home. A passage of Scripture wouldn't escape Amy's mind. It was 1 Corinthians 3:12-14:

"If anyone builds on this foundation using gold, silver, costly stones, wood, hay or straw, their work will be shown for what it is, because the Day will bring it to light. It will be revealed with fire, and the fire will test the quality of each person's work. If what has been built survives…"

The words became so real that Amy turned to see who had spoken them. She saw nothing. She knew it had been the voice of God.

That afternoon, Amy did some serious soul-searching. She determined in her heart to follow Jesus, even if it meant forsaking the luxury and beauty she enjoyed. It was no small sacrifice to embrace this journey of all-in discipleship. Still, from that moment on, she wholeheartedly embraced Jesus and committed to be "dead to the world and its applause, to all its customs, fashions, and laws."

Amy began to reach out to the "shawlies," girls who worked in the local mills. They were dubbed shawlies, because they were too poor to buy hats and therefore covered their heads with shawls. Shawlies were somehow offensive to "proper" church members. Amy's newfound love for God and others began to cause irritation. Some church members were appalled that Amy would bring such "common" girls into the church. Amy, having been "crucified with Christ," no longer cared about her reputation. She knew God was at work and continued to bring the girls.

Church members soon changed their attitude when the shawlies began coming in large numbers. The ministry outgrew the church building, and Amy began searching for a new place to minister to the girls. Amy was only twenty-two, but she trusted God to lead her. God did. He provided land and a building, and The Mill and Factory Girls' Branch of the YWCA was opened in 1889.

The grand opening was about putting God on display, not Amy. A banner proclaimed, "That in all things He might have the preeminence." Others led the service. Amy wasn't even on the platform. Though it was her vision that initiated the ministry and her dream that made the building possible, she sat inconspicuously in the middle of the audience and sought no recognition. Amy Carmichael continued to die to self.

After much fruitful ministry in Ireland, Amy heard God's call to go overseas. Many discouraged and even chastised her for it. Continuing to listen to God's voice alone, she went. Amy ministered briefly in China, but settled in India, where she shared the gospel and rescued children from prostitution in Hindu temples. Amy grappled with her ministry to children. After all, some considered it "less important or profitable" work. Gradually, Amy's heart and mind found peace. She saw great value in offering herself to God in whatever He put her to doing, including serving as mother to His children.

Over and again, Amy refused to question God. Each question was a chance to die, to be reminded of Christ's lordship in her life. "He held all the rights. She had turned them over long ago to Him when she resolved to follow Him to the uttermost," said Elisabeth Elliot in her biography of Amy. "It was one more way of saying no to herself and yes to God."

Amy spent the remaining fifty-three years of her life serving in India. Her heart and devotion in setting up orphanages and ministering to people she met kept her gaze and focus on Jesus and not herself. Her standards were high for the cause of Christ. She often warned against "half-hearted missionaries." Only workers prepared to die to self and live for Christ would do.

Amy once received a letter from a girl who was considering overseas missions. The girl asked, "What is missionary life like?" Amy responded simply, "Missionary life is a chance to die."

Amy's Significant Contribution
Amy Carmichael's life and ministry reflected God's love and care for orphans, widows, and outcasts. She personified selflessness and humility by allowing Christ to determine the desires of her heart. For Amy, that meant rejecting the luxuries and comforts of her life in Ireland to become "mother" to children in India who desperately needed her. God employed Amy to rescue thousands of children and give them hope in Christ. The Dohnavur Fellowship, which she founded, continues to impact lives today.

Recommended Reading

A Chance to Die, The Life and Legacy of Amy Carmichael, by Elisabeth Elliot

Notable Quote
"A crucified life cannot be self-assertive. The cup that is full of sweet water cannot spill bitter-tasting drops, however sharply it is knocked."

IT'S MY TURN TO ...

ENGAGE THE STORY

Amy and her brothers automatically helped an elderly lady with her load because they knew it was the right thing to do. She didn't question their actions until she saw the disapproving looks they received from other people. How much do the opinions of others matter to you? Are there service opportunities that you may be missing out on because you are worried about what others might think, or afraid of feeling the shame that Amy experienced?

GOD USED Amy's experience as a teenager to beckon her to a life of all-in discipleship. That day she chose to live her life saying "yes" to God. What are some examples you saw of Amy "dying to self?" How can emulate those in your life?

ENGAGE GOD'S WORD

AMY DID NOT HESITATE to deny herself because she knew God was not asking her to do anything that had not already been done for her. Read Luke 9:22-26. What does Jesus require from those who want to be His disciples?

. . .

It's My Turn

SOME CONSIDERED Amy's work with children in India as "less important or profitable." A turning point in Amy's life came when she was reminded of the words of 1 Corinthians 3:12-14. Look at that passage and Acts 20:24. What determines what Kingdom work is significant and worthwhile? What race has God set before you right now?

ENGAGE MY LIFE

AMY SAID, "A crucified life cannot be self-assertive. The cup that is full of sweet water cannot spill bitter-tasting drops, however sharply it is knocked." Amy served joyfully and it overflowed to those around her. What would you say is filling up your life? And what is overflowing from your life to those around you?

WHEN AMY GAVE GOD HER "YES," He opened her eyes to see the "shawlies," the undervalued in her own neighborhood. Later she became a mother to the unloved children of India. Ask God to open your eyes to the undervalued and unloved people in your own hometown and beyond. As He does, how does He want you to deny yourself and love them this week?

FOR FURTHER REFLECTION & ENGAGEMENT

WHAT DID I learn from Amy Carmichael's life and story?

DID Amy's story stir something in me I need to pay attention to and talk to God about?

. . .

What clear, measurable "next step" should I take in response to what God is showing me?

Who in the Kingdom community will I ask to encourage me in this and keep me accountable?

Why this lesson, this day? What's God up to in deepening my faith and multiplying His Kingdom?

9

JOHN HYDE (1865-1912)

DECLARATION 9 – IT'S MY TURN TO INTERCEDE IN PRAYER FOR THE SPIRITUALLY LOST

Because of his perseverance in prayer, the people of India called John Hyde "the man who never sleeps." He was slow of speech, slightly hearing impaired, and mild-mannered. But his steadfast commitment to the power of prayer taught and encouraged many that prayer is the driving force behind God's work.

Just before the turn of the twentieth century, John sensed a call to minister to an unreached people group in the nation of India. He was one of only five missionaries to serve in the Punjab region. They were often rejected and mistreated in the early years. Very few people came to Christ. John realized the only way he would make it was to rely on the power of prayer. He began to lead his fellow missionaries in intercession for the nation of India. In 1899, he began spending entire nights in prayer. He would work all day, then labor in prayer all night. Prayer for the lost became his passion, and his sole, "secret weapon" for ministry.

In 1904, John attended the first of what would become an annual convention for Indian Christians and Western missionaries. He helped form the Punjab Prayer Union to support the convention, convincing his fellow workers that nothing could happen for the Kingdom of God apart from intercessory prayer. The workers had seen so little fruit that they were easily convinced of this truth.

By the second year of the convention, John had gained a reputation as a man of prayer. He spent many days and nights in the prayer room, strengthened and sustained by God. As he prayed, he often became so heavy-hearted for the sins of the world and of the Church that he would burst into tears. A friend of his once wrote, "He missed many meals, and when I went to his room, I would find him lying as in great agony, or walking up and down as if an inward fire were burning in his bones." John often went without sleep and food. Yet, John was joyful and energetic—not despite it, rather because of it. "One thought was constantly uppermost in his mind," his friend wrote, "that our Lord still agonizes for souls."

In 1908, John dared to pray for what many considered an impossible request. He asked God for one soul per day to be won to Christ. Though most of the other workers could not fathom such results, he proceeded with his bold request. By the next year, over four hundred people had been won to Christ!

During the 1909 convention, John made a new prayer goal: to double the number of souls won. It seemed impossible again. This time, however, his fellow Christians joined him in prayer. Sure enough, by the next convention, over eight hundred souls had been won for Christ! In that convention, he courageously determined to double the goal again. He prayed with unquenchable passion: "O, God, give me souls or I die!"

The new goal met; John rightly earned the nickname "Praying Hyde." He began to travel about, inviting other workers and nationals to pray for the lost in India.

While in Calcutta, John's health began to fail. Some of his friends convinced him to see a doctor. He did, and the diagnosis was highly unusual. The doctor discovered John's heart had shifted from one side of his chest to the other. Years of passionate prayer had affected his frail body.

The doctor gave him strict instructions to get complete rest for

It's My Turn

several months or he would die. But "Praying Hyde" could not fathom slowing down his prayer life. Continuing his passionate ministry of intercession, John lived two more years. In that span, he saw a wave of unprecedented conversions in that part of the world.

John left India in 1911 for England. While there, he attended an evangelistic meeting he felt burdened to pray for. Later, Dr. J. Wilbur Chapman, one of the speakers, wrote:

The audience was extremely small, results seemed impossible, but I received a note saying that an American missionary was coming to the town and was going to pray God's blessing upon our work. He was known as "Praying Hyde."

Almost instantly the tide turned. The hall was packed, and my first invitation meant fifty men for Jesus Christ. As we were leaving, I said, "Mr. Hyde, I want you to pray for me."

He came to my room…dropped on his knees, waited five minutes without a single syllable coming from his lips. Then with upturned face, down which the tears were streaming, he said: "Oh, God!"

Then for five minutes at least, he was still again. Then, his arm went around my shoulder and there came up from the depth of his heart such petitions for men as I had never heard before. I rose from my knees to know what real prayer was.

Although feeble and infirmed, John continued his ministry of intercessory prayer to the time of his death.

Today, "Praying Hyde" stands as a testimony—not to the power of gifts and intellect—but to the power of the Holy Spirit to do "immeasurably more than all we ask or imagine" when we intercede in prayer.

John's Significant Contribution

John Hyde's missionary methods underscore the truth that prayer is the driving force behind evangelism (if not all things). Like the early apostles, John recognized that time in prayer and study of the Scriptures could not be compromised by other seemingly worthwhile activities. He pursued God's heart for the lost and interceded for thousands to enter the Kingdom of heaven.

Recommended Reading
John Hyde, by Francis McGraw

Notable Quote
"0, God, give me souls or I die!"

IT'S MY TURN TO ...

ENGAGE THE STORY

John was slow of speech, slightly hearing impaired, and mild-mannered. Some would say he didn't have the skill set to serve God's Kingdom effectively. What did John believe was his "secret weapon" for ministry? How much time did he devote to this?

LOOK BACK at the beginning of the story. What kind of response did the missionaries receive from the people in India? How much of a change occurred when John began to challenge them to rely on prayer as their weapon of choice in battle? Have you relied on prayer in this way?

ENGAGE GOD'S WORD

JOHN'S PRAYER for at least one person to commit his or her life to Christ every day seemed impossible. God, however, exceeded that prayer-laden goal and brought over 400! Read Ephesians 3:14-21. Why might it be valuable to pray for things that seem out of reach or farfetched?

READ LUKE 19:1-10. There was a point in John's life where he realized that "our Lord still agonizes for souls." What does your heart agonize for? Is it in alignment with God's heart? Why or why not?

ENGAGE MY LIFE

AT AGE SEVENTEEN, John discovered that the purpose of prayer is not to get from God what we want, but to allow God to receive from us what He wants. Look back at Dr. Chapman's experience praying with John. What do you think was happening in those long moments of silence? How much time do you spend listening in prayer for what God's wants? Stop now and spend some time in silence before the Lord.

JOHN OFTEN MISSED meals in order to spend more time praying for lost souls. Think of a lost friend or family member as well as an unreached people group (you can research people groups at JoshuaProject.net). Consider setting aside times to fast and pray that they would come to know Jesus.

IN A JOURNAL, START A "PRAYER REQUEST" section and an "answered prayer" section. Record prayers and answers. Praise and thank God as you write.

FOR FURTHER REFLECTION & ENGAGEMENT

WHAT DID I learn from John Hyde's life and story?

DID John's story stir something in me I need to pay attention to and talk to God about?

. . .

What clear, measurable "next step" should I take in response to what God is showing me?

Who in the Kingdom community will I ask to encourage me in this and keep me accountable?

Why this lesson, this day? What's God up to in deepening my faith and multiplying His Kingdom?

10

WILLIAM WILBERFORCE (1759-1833)

DECLARATION 10 – IT'S MY TURN TO PERSEVERE IN LIFE AND LOVE

William Wilberforce is widely known and revered as a champion in the abolition movement in England. His life, however, wasn't always pointed that direction. In the earlier years of his political career, William aspired to be popular and powerful. His charm and eloquence brought great admiration among his peers and fast-tracked him toward political success. Although William had grown up with plenty of exposure to the gospel, the opinions of others far outweighed any desire to follow Jesus. William was "afraid to surrender to Christ for fear of what others might say." Christianity seemed more of a hindrance than a political help.

That all changed when William came to what he called a crisis of the soul. "I am afraid of turning my back on Christ," he said, "but I also fear losing face and prestige. If my constituents were to hear that I embraced religion, my career would be over." William struggled with those fears over a two-year span (1785-86). Inner wrestling and reflection led to conviction and grace, and William committed his life to Jesus.

Initially, William considered leaving politics to enter vocational ministry, but John Newton discouraged the idea. "Imagine what [God] can do through a gifted member of Parliament," he said. "There's nothing in the Bible that says you cannot be both a Christian and a statesman." William agreed and continued his political life under Christ's governance and not his own.

William was eager and vocal about his new life in Christ, including when he spoke in Parliament. At first, talking about his faith in Jesus and how Scripture informed various legislative decisions brought ridicule from his colleagues. Eventually, they began to respect William for his passionate beliefs and consistent living that validated his testimony. In time, William found a new calling and sense of purpose as an activist against slavery. "God Almighty has set before me two great objects," he said, "the suppression of the Slave Trade and the reformation of manners."

William began with the second of the "two great objects" by developing a "Society for the Suppression of Vice." People enjoyed their vices, however, more than being told what not to do, and the "society" was met by scorn and opposition. William didn't give up. In 1793, When the East India Company's charter was up for renewal, he proposed another idea: a resolution to allow missionaries to travel to India. That proposal was rejected as well.

William returned his focus to the first of the "two great objects" and began to concentrate on slavery. Throughout the 1700s, the slave trade in the British Empire had been viewed as a "necessary evil." By 1787, however, some began to see the slave trade simply as evil, and several abolitionists formed a Committee for the Abolition of the Slave Trade. Though well-organized, the group needed a strong voice in Parliament. William was the perfect candidate. He was influential and independent, an eloquent speaker with a quick mind. William consented to be that voice. Later in life, he expressed the reasons why he did: "So enormous, so dreadful, so irremediable did the trade's wickedness appear that my own mind was completely made up for abolition. Let the consequences be what they would: I from this time determined that I would never rest until I had effected its abolition."

In 1789, William addressed Parliament with a three-hour speech on abolition. He described the capture of slaves and the ocean passage

It's My Turn

they faced. He then introduced the first motion to abolish slave trade. Debate on the bill began in 1791. Unfortunately, William's opponents prevailed, and the bill was rejected.

William tried again a year later. He pleaded for the slaves he so desperately wanted to receive freedom. "Africa! Africa!" he cried, "Your sufferings have been the theme that has arrested and engaged my heart. Your sufferings no tongue can express; no language impart."

By 1792, William had become such a prominent opponent of slavery that officers in the West Indies Regiments threatened his life. John Wesley, the founder of Methodism, wrote to encourage William: "Unless God has raised you up for this very thing, you will be worn out by the opposition of men and devils. But if God be for you, who can be against you? Be not weary of well-doing. Go on in the name of God, and in the power of his might, till even American slavery, the vilest that ever saw the sun, shall vanish away before it."

William pressed on. Over the next seventeen years, abolitionists moved the conversation beyond Parliament to the streets. They sought to expose slavery's plight, obtain petitions, and bring about legislative change. Their successes were minimal. Vested interests, filibusters, bigotry, international politics, and slave unrest brought heavy opposition and mistreatment by pro-slavery activists.

William didn't quit. Finally, in 1807, nearly twenty years after William first introduced the issue to Parliament, the House of Commons voted by a huge majority to abolish the slave trade in the British Empire. It was a day of great triumph.

The celebration, however, didn't last long. God had more work for William to do. Though trading new slaves was now illegal, owning slaves was not. William and his colleagues began working to ensure enforcement of the slave trade law and to eventually abolish slavery altogether. Like abolishing slave trade, it was a long, drawn-out fight.

By 1817, William had set his sights on the emancipation of all slaves. Unfortunately, age and illness slowed his ability to champion the cause the way he once was able. Another sixteen years of battling finally paid off. In 1833, William got his opportunity in Parliament to speak for the total abolition of slavery. And, after forty-five years as a politician, William Wilberforce saw the vision God gave him fulfilled. On July 26, 1833, just four days before his death, Parliament passed the Bill for the Abolition of Slavery in all British territories.

William's Significant Contribution
William Wilberforce led the long and arduous crusade to end the practice of slavery in the British Empire, which paved the way for the end of slavery in America. His perseverance paid off. God used William's unique platform as a politician to set people free.

Recommended Reading
Amazing Grace: William Wilberforce and the Heroic Campaign to End Slavery, by Eric Metaxas

Notable Quote
"My walk is a public one. My business is in the world, and I must mix in the assemblies of men or quit the post which Providence seems to have assigned me."

IT'S MY TURN TO …

ENGAGE THE STORY

William assumed that that his "career would be over" if he surrendered his life to Christ. However, God intended to use William right where he was, by simply changing his focus. In what ways might God want to shift your focus and use you right where you are, for His glory?

WILLIAM PERSEVERED through many long years of what might have seemed like a hopeless battle. Have you faced any "hopeless battles"? What's encouraged you during those struggles?

ENGAGE GOD'S WORD

Have you joined God's unique Kingdom mission in your life, right where you are? William did so as he took note of God's heart for the world's great needs. Read Matthew 6:10. So much of our world is still not as it should be; so we pray and labor to see more of His "Kingdom come and will be done on earth as it is in heaven." In what ways have you noticed that our world needs more of God's Kingdom? Ask God to open your eyes to see the brokenness and needs of the world and to take a bold stand where needed.

Are you confidently persevering in the task God has placed before you or have you joined "those who shrink back"? Why or why not? Read Hebrews 10:32-39 and 2 Corinthians 4:16-18. How can these passages encourage us to continue running the race? Memorize 1-2 of these verses this week.

ENGAGE MY LIFE

It took 45 years, right up until his death, before William saw the vision God gave him fulfilled. When it comes to completing the tasks God has placed before you, how long do you feel is too long to persevere? William counted each victory as a steppingstone to the final destination. How can you practice seeing and praising God for the smaller victories that come along the journey?

What is one conviction that you know you have compromised on because it was too hard or too lonely or too radical? Talk to God about why you compromised. Confess any places where you failed to trust His plan, power, or provision. Ask a friend to walk with you, encourage you, and pray for you as you continue the work God has placed before you.

FOR FURTHER REFLECTION & ENGAGEMENT

WHAT DID I learn from William Wilberforce's life and story?

DID William's story stir something in me I need to pay attention to and talk to God about?

WHAT CLEAR, MEASURABLE "NEXT STEP" should I take in response to what God is showing me?

WHO IN THE Kingdom community will I ask to encourage me in this and keep me accountable?

WHY THIS LESSON, this day? What's God up to in deepening my faith and multiplying His Kingdom?

PART II

IT'S MY TURN TO LIVE A LIFE ON PURPOSE

11

SUSANNA WESLEY (1669-1742)

DECLARATION 11 – IT'S MY TURN TO EMBRACE MY UNIQUE
ROLE IN GOD'S KINGDOM

Susanna Wesley provides living proof that fame and high-profile ministry status aren't necessary for advancing God's Kingdom in significant ways. Susanna gave birth to nineteen children in twenty-one years. Sadly, nine of the children died in infancy. The remaining ten children grew to become strong men and women of God; the two most notable being John, the itinerant preacher, and Charles, the musician. Susanna devoted her life to raising, nurturing, and discipling her children, and her unique Kingdom contribution continues to impact countless others for the Kingdom in ever widening, domino-ripple-effect ways.

Susanna was raised in London, herself the 25th of 25 children. She married the Reverend Samuel Wesley, and they began pastoring a church in a more rural part of England where things were culturally different than Samuel or Susanna were accustomed. Samuel struggled with country life. He also had deficiencies in managing business affairs and family finances. His mismanagement of money caused pain and hardship for Susanna and the kids. Out of necessity, Susanna managed their financial resources in addition to caring for many other family needs. To her credit, she did so gracefully without embarrassing or shaming Samuel.

At age twenty-one, Susanna gave birth to her first child. That was the beginning of the next 30+ years of devotion and care to the upbringing of her children. Her purpose was clear: "There is nothing I now desire to live for but to do some small service to my children," she said, "that as I have brought them into the world, I may, if it please God, be an instrument of doing good to their souls." Susanna kept her promise, as did God to her.

Her commitment to raising, teaching, and disciplining her children came with great sacrifice to herself. For Susanna, the cost was well worth it. She wrote, "No one can, without renouncing the world, in the most literal sense, observe my method; and there are few, if any, that would entirely devote above twenty years of the prime of life in hopes to save the souls of their children, which they think may be saved without so much ado; for that was my principal intention, however unskillfully and unsuccessfully managed."

Education in the early 1700s most often came at the expense of a hired tutor. The Wesley's couldn't afford one. Susanna began educating her children at home. Susanna loved to learn. Most women weren't formally educated in Susanna's day, but she had the rare gift of having been educated by her father. Susanna was generous with her gift, and she cultivated a love of learning in her kids. Having little money for textbooks, Susanna got creative. She taught from library books, the Bible, and material she wrote herself. She even developed a manual for religious instruction.

Susanna was firm with her children, but she was equally patient. Once, as Samuel observed Susanna repeating the same lesson to one of the children again and again, he grew impatient. He exclaimed, "I wonder at your patience! You have told that child twenty times the same thing." Susanna replied, "If I had satisfied myself by mentioning it only nineteen times, I should have lost all my labor. It was the twentieth time that crowned it."

Susanna's Kingdom contribution went beyond educator and disciplinarian. She was also a mentor and friend. For years, Susanna scheduled weekly, one-on-one time with every child. Once her children left home, she faithfully corresponded with them through frequent letters.

It's My Turn

The writings of her sons John and Charles are filled with examples of how much value they placed on her counsel and guidance.

While raising ten children consumed most of Susanna's time, she placed a high priority on her relationship with God. She made it her rule "never to spend more time in any matter of mere recreation in one day than spent in private religious duties." Susanna knew that to serve others and love well required up-close time with God. She gave great priority to times of solitude with the Lord every morning and evening. Along with prayer and study, she practiced intimate times with God in everyday tasks and conversations. She wrote, "Religion is not to be confined to the church or closet, nor exercised only in prayer and meditation, but everywhere I am in His presence."

In Samuel's frequent absence, Susanna also directed the farming of their land, managed financial matters, and oversaw the church. She also led times of worship with the children in her kitchen. The children would sing psalms, read prayers, and listen to short sermons from Samuel's library. Soon, others joined the gathering. Word of the gathering spread, and more than two hundred people began attending!

Susanna accomplished a great deal in her lifetime. Her crowning contribution, however, did not place her in the limelight. She was content to nurture, teach, and guide her children to love God and others well. Her Kingdom contribution is not best seen in her life but in the fruitfulness of her children's lives, particularly John and Charles. John was very close to his mother. He called her the greatest influence in his life. The self-examination and methodical practice of holiness he saw in his mother's life became hallmarks of the Methodist movement he founded. Charles wrote more than 6,000 hymns, many still sung in worship all around the world.

Susanna's final request as she lay dying was a simple one: "Children," she said, "as soon as I am released, sing a psalm of praise to God." And they did. To the end of her life, Susanna Wesley glorified God and served others. She contributed to God's Kingdom in ways unnoticed by many but everlastingly evident to God.

Susanna's Significant Contribution

Susanna Wesley raised nine children in an atmosphere of love, discipline and godliness. She devoted her life to the intellectual and spiritual education of her children, seeking to produce a generation of her family who would follow Christ devotedly. Her son Charles is considered one of the greatest hymn writers of all time, and her son John founded the Methodist church movement. Susanna has also been called the "Mother of Methodism" because John modeled much of the Methodist movement after practices he learned from her.

Recommended Reading
Susanna Wesley: The Mother of John & Charles Wesley, by Arnold A. Dallimore

50 Women Every Christian Should Know: Learning from Heroines of the Faith, by Michelle DeRusha

Seven Women: And the Secret of Their Greatness, by Eric Metaxas

Notable Quote
"I am content to fill a little space if God be glorified."

IT'S MY TURN TO …

ENGAGE THE STORY

Susanna believed her life's purpose was to nurture, teach, and guide her children to love God and others well. How do you think her belief would be viewed in today's culture—admired and respected, looked down upon, considered successful? Why?

JOHN AND CHARLES WESLEY impacted millions throughout their lives. Their greatest influence was their mother, an ordinary Kingdom Laborer who fulfilled her unique purpose. Who has been the most influential person in your life? What do you admire about them? How

It's My Turn

has this person helped shape you? Was it a famous person, or someone you knew well? (If you are going through these questions as a group take note of how many people were impacted by a famous person vs. an everyday person? What do these numbers tell you about the impact of everyday people embracing their unique role in God's kingdom?)

ENGAGE GOD'S WORD

READ EPHESIANS 2:10. How does your perspective on life change knowing that God has prepared good works in advance for you to do? Now, take a look at Colossians 3:16-17. What are some expressions of these good works in your life?

READ 2 Timothy 1:5 and Acts 4:13. What does God Word teach us about ordinary people embracing unique Kingdom roles? Why is Susanna's role as a mother just as crucially important and valuable to God's Kingdom mission as her sons who labored as Christian leaders (itinerant evangelist and worship leader)? Have you always thought this way, or is your perspective being shifted by the Scriptures and Susanna's story?

ENGAGE MY LIFE

SUSANNA'S KINGDOM contributions were ones that went unnoticed by many. However, she was "content to fill a little space, if God be glorified." Prioritizing her relationship with God enabled Susanna to embrace her unique role in God's kingdom. Where does your personal time with God fall on your priority list?

. . .

Take a few moments to brainstorm what unique and distinct ministry might look like in your life. What interests has God given you? Burdens or passions? Talents? Skills? Training or experiences? What do you just naturally enjoy doing? Visit ForgeForward.org/Resources and download the "Personal Ministry Inventory" to further brainstorm your YOUnique ministry.

FOR FURTHER REFLECTION & ENGAGEMENT

What did I learn from Susanna Wesley's life and story?

Did Susanna's story stir something in me I need to pay attention to and talk to God about?

What clear, measurable "next step" should I take in response to what God is showing me?

Who in the Kingdom community will I ask to encourage me in this and keep me accountable?

Why this lesson, this day? What's God up to in deepening my faith and multiplying His Kingdom?

12

ERIC LIDDELL (1902-1945)

DECLARATION 12 – IT'S MY TURN TO USE MY GOD-GIVEN GIFTS FOR HIS GLORY

Eric Liddell was a runner—to the glory of God. What he did with his feet amazed and astonished the world.

Born in China as the son of Scottish missionaries, Eric knew from the time he was a child that he wanted to follow in his father's mission work. But Eric also excelled at sports. His athletic talents were numerous, the greatest among them was speed. Eric could run. His many childhood trophies and ribbons proved it. Though athletically successful, Eric intended to abandon sports once he began college in Scotland. That changed when a persuasive friend talked him into participating on the track team. It wasn't long until Eric discovered he had an opportunity to glorify God with his athletic talents.

Eric gained national fame and was chosen to represent Great Britain at the 1924 Olympic games. The growing publicity somewhat embarrassed Eric. His joy was in running and competing not accolades. He preferred to give attention and attribute the success to his team, university, or country. His approach kept him winning in a multitude of ways.

By the time Eric reached the 1924 Olympics in Paris, he was favored to win the 100-meter dash. To everyone's astonishment, however, he withdrew from the race just after the schedule was released. The race was slated to be run on Sunday. Eric felt strongly Sundays were holy and should be set apart for rest and worship.

It created quite a stir. Some suggested Eric could make a rare exception and God would understand. Others recommended petitioning to change the day of the race. While Eric was disappointed, his conviction held. He quietly withdrew from the races to be held that day.

Because Eric had been Great Britain's best hope for a medal, team leaders decided to enter him in a different event: the 400-meter run. Most thought his chances as a 100-meter sprinter were slim in such a long race. That didn't bother Eric or the God who made him fast. Eric shocked the world by winning the gold medal in world-record time!

For Eric, running wasn't about excitement and medals. Racing was a way to bring glory to God. When his sister tried to persuade him to enter missionary work sooner than planned, Eric said, "I believe that God made me for a purpose—for China. But He also made me fast, and when I run, I feel His pleasure. To give it up would be to hold Him in contempt. You were right, it's not just fun. To win is to honor Him."

Paying homage to his injured teammate who had previously been Great Britain's best hope for the 400-meter race, Eric stated "In the dust of defeat as well as the laurels of victory, there is a glory to be found if one has done his best."

Eric continued to discover ways to reflect Jesus in his life but was often reluctant to share about his faith publicly. Sensing God was giving him a platform through his Olympic fame, he gladly accepted when leaders of a local evangelistic crusade asked Eric to speak. They knew the famous athlete would draw big crowds. They were right. The event became one of many crusades through which Eric used his talent and accolades of running to share about the goodness and glory of God.

Before long, the time came for Eric to pursue God's calling to serve as a missionary to China. Within weeks after returning from Paris, Eric chose a luncheon as the platform to announce his new direction.

As with most events Eric attended, he was asked to give a speech. After thanking many who had contributed to his athletic success, the crowd applauded at what appeared to be the end of Eric's speech. But Eric did not sit down as expected. The smile on his face faded, and the audience sensed his serious tone. He announced that he had been offered a teaching position at a university in Tientsin, China and explained he would be devoting the entirety of his life to missions.

Eric stood before the audience as a young, intelligent, world-class athlete with more opportunities for fame, prosperity and success than most of them would ever know. But they should not have been surprised. Eric once again showed the world he was a person of principle. Neither public opinion nor the lure of success could sway him from the call of God. Eric had made a decision, his life was surrendered, and his future belonged to God and His plans.

In 1924, Eric asked for and received a one-year deferment on his teaching assignment in China. He used the time to study theology, travel, and speak. Eric was happy to share his story as well as God's in whatever venue people gathered. Scores of people came to Christ in theaters, churches, dance halls, and social clubs.

At age twenty-three, just one year after he had captured the attention of the world as an Olympic champion, Eric headed to China. Eric's impact in China was just as powerful as his influence back home. When his students at the Anglo-Chinese College found out their teacher was famous in his home country, they sought to understand why he would abandon such success and fame in order to come to China. His fast feet and unswerving commitment to God left many in China with one conclusion: the God Eric serves is strong, authentic, and worth following.

Eric Liddell died of a brain tumor while being held captive in a Japanese internment camp during World War II. His life was documented in the Academy Award-winning film Chariots of Fire. Eric used the unique gifts, opportunities, and influences of his life to put God on display. Like the apostle Paul, Eric could confidently proclaim at the conclusion of his life, "I have fought the good fight, I have finished the race, I have kept the faith" (2 Timothy 4:7).

Eric's Significant Contribution

As an Olympic athlete, Eric Liddell used his talents for the glory of God. He honored God by using his platform of athletics to draw people to Christ. He laid aside this world's fame and fortune to pursue God's greater call and delight—for Eric, that was China. His life demonstrates that a laborer's activities don't require a typical vocational ministry approach. God uses the uniqueness of every laborer.

Recommended Reading

Eric Liddell, by Catherine Swift

Notable Quote

"I believe that God made me for a purpose—for China. But He also made me fast, and when I run, I feel His pleasure. To give it up would be to hold Him in contempt."

IT'S MY TURN TO …

ENGAGE THE STORY

Eric wrote, "Ask yourself: If I know something to be true, am I prepared to follow it, even though it is contrary to what I want?... Will I follow it if it means being laughed at, if it means personal financial loss or some kind of hardship?" Although Eric faced criticism for choosing not to run on Sunday, how do we see that God honored his decision? Looking back, do you think Eric was pleased with his decision?

ERIC NEVER WAVERED from the call to serve in China but chose to make the most of every opportunity God gave him no matter where he stepped foot. How did Eric's integrity and his unique gift of running glorify God even in China?

ENGAGE GOD'S WORD

READ 2 TIMOTHY 4:1-8. How was Eric "prepared in every season" to glorify God and make Him known in word and in deed? How would this look in your life?

READ HEBREWS 11:24-26 and Hebrews 12:1-3. Eric lived out these truths as he showed the world that his eternal priorities were more important than temporal opportunities. How can we do the same, joyfully pressing forward in running our race? Where have your eyes and attention been fixed recently?

ENGAGE MY LIFE

ERIC SAW his ability to run as useful for advancing God's Kingdom. We are all born with God-given gifts, skills, and passions. What are yours? And how might you use them most effectively to further glorify God and advance His kingdom?

WHEN ERIC'S students in China found out their humble teacher rejected fame in order to teach, they came to the conclusion that he served a strong, authentic, and worthy God. Using our gifts for God's glory should point other's attention to the giver of all good things (James 1:17). Who would you say currently receives the most praise through your life and gifts: you, God, or someone else? How can this shift to glorify God more and more?

FOR FURTHER REFLECTION & ENGAGEMENT

WHAT DID I learn from Eric Liddell's life and story?

. . .

DID Eric's story stir something in me I need to pay attention to and talk to God about?

WHAT CLEAR, MEASURABLE "NEXT STEP" should I take in response to what God is showing me?

WHO IN THE Kingdom community will I ask to encourage me in this and keep me accountable?

WHY THIS LESSON, this day? What's God up to in deepening my faith and multiplying His Kingdom?

13

MARTIN LUTHER (1483-1546)

DECLARATION 13 – IT'S MY TURN TO STAND FOR GOD'S TRUTH

The offer to recant, to take back all the things he'd said and written, must have been tempting for Martin Luther as he stood before the Diet of Worms in April of 1521. After all, Martin was just a common monk. How had he come to stand before Charles V, the emperor of Germany, to be tried for treason and heresy? As a monk and a priest in the Roman Catholic church, Martin wearied his priest with confessions, constant scathing self-examinations, and personal punishments. He was constantly concerned that he was not forgiven for his sins. One day, God changed all that. Martin was reading the letter to the Romans and Romans 1:17 leapt off the page at him. For the first time he realized salvation is by faith alone, not by our works and goodness. That truth discovery opposed the teaching of his time, a teaching which still exists today in both overt and subtle forms.

As his understanding and theology developed, Martin became concerned with materialistic corruption, legalism, and a lack of spiritual care in the church. His concerns led him to write 95 Theses (dissenting arguments) and tack the document to the church door in Wittenberg, Germany. Through the years, some have described that day as a rebellious act. While it did begin something radical, Martin was most likely practicing a common means of inviting further theological dialogue and debate. Whatever the tone of his tacking, Martin's 95 Theses and subsequent writings gave birth to the Reformation movement.

Following the 95 Theses posting in 1517, Martin continued to write and speak for reform within the Catholic Church. His ideas rapidly gained approval among the common people of Germany, who were frustrated with the lack of spiritual care, materialistic corruption, and political maneuvering of the Church. In all the controversy, Martin never viewed himself as a rebel, but believed he was simply keeping his vow to teach and defend the scriptures.

Martin, a monk for over ten years, had devoted himself to the study and teaching of scripture and prayer when he acknowledged his true conversion in 1518. It was then that the simplicity of Romans 1:17 became apparent to him. Faith in Jesus Christ alone fully meets the demand for righteousness the law requires. Jesus Christ, God's perfect righteousness, is enough to atone for the sin that separates us relationally from God.

In 1521, facing increased pressure from Pope Leo X to recant under the threat of excommunication, Martin wrote three eye-opening papers. The first two exposed the misuse of power by church leaders and the access denied everyday believers to serve God's Kingdom freely.

The third paper, "On the Freedom of the Christian," argued against the church's misleading teaching of the day that religious rule-keeping and good behavior can somehow bridge the gap our sin creates between us and God. Our faith in Jesus and His redeeming work on the Cross, Martin proclaimed, is the only way that leads to our relationship with God being restored. Said succinctly, "by faith alone."

By January 1521, Martin was considered an outlaw of the Holy Roman Empire and had been excommunicated by the Roman Catholic church. Emperor Charles V called for an imperial diet (trial) to convene at Worms and determine Martin's fate.

It's My Turn

As the trial began, Martin was shown a large pile of books and asked, "Did you write these books?" After stating that he had, Martin was asked, "Will you now take back all the things you said in these books?" Martin asked for time to consider the question. The emperor consented and allowed Martin 24 hours to respond.

The next day, a large crowd gathered for the trial. The meeting was moved to a larger hall, but so packed was the new venue that some were turned away. Martin was asked the question again. Although the exact words of his reply have been debated, he is reported to have said, "Unless I am convinced, by scripture or by plain reason... I cannot and will not recant. It is neither safe nor right to go against one's conscience. Here I stand. I cannot do otherwise. God help me." His statement sent shockwaves through the audience as the listeners added their own opinions to the chaos.

The fear of revolt by the people of Germany led even the strongest opposers of Martin to appeal to the emperor for a continued private hearing by a committee. Three days of questioning and appeals for Martin to change his stand were unsuccessful. He would not be moved.

Years later, Martin wrote that the thought which consumed him most during his trial was not that he was being tried by an emperor, but that both he and the emperor would have to answer to God. The desire to stand unashamed before his heavenly Father gave Martin strength to stand unwavering before the earthly emperor. God and His Word was Martin Luther's final authority.

Martin's Significant Contribution
Martin Luther's 95 Theses, tacked to the Wittenberg Chapel door, summarized his protest against the corruption in the Church and ushered in the Protestant Reformation of the early sixteenth century. His dedication to making God's truth accessible to all people provided incredible momentum to translating the Bible into the common German vernacular of the day.

Recommended Reading
Here I Stand: A Life of Martin Luther, by Roland Bainton.

Martin Luther, by Eric Metaxas.

Notable Quote
"I own but one thing, my own unworthy body. ...If they choose to take it... they will but make me poorer by one or two hours of life. The sweet Redeemer, my Lord Jesus Christ, is enough for me, to whom I shall sing as long as I live. And if anyone is unwilling to sing with me, then what is that to me."

IT'S MY TURN TO ...

ENGAGE THE STORY

Early on, Luther was tormented with the fear that he had not been forgiven of his sins. What brought transformation to Luther's heart and life? How does the story of Luther's life show us that taking God at His word brings conviction and boldness?

ONCE LUTHER'S eyes were off himself and fixed on Christ, he began speaking bolding for the sake of the welfare of the body of Christ. At his trial, Luther said, "Unless I am convinced by the testimony of Scripture or by clear reason... I cannot and will not recant anything, since to act against one's conscience is neither safe nor right. I cannot do otherwise. Here I stand, may God help me." What was the driving force behind Luther's actions? What motivated him to boldly speak out in the ways he did?

ENGAGE GOD'S WORD

It's My Turn

READ JOHN 8:31-32. How do you see reality of these verses in Luther's life? What are some things that Luther's freedom, resulting from God's truth, compelled him to do?

READ 2 Peter 1:20-21 and 2 Timothy 3:16-17. Luther faced criticism for his teaching of Scripture alone, faith alone, grace alone, Christ alone, to God's glory alone. Luther had been held in captivity by the lie that salvation partly relies on tradition, our good works, and the church structure but was transformed by Scripture. Are there any areas of your life where you find yourself held captive? Take a few minutes to ask God what lies you are believing and to reveal the truth of His word.

ENGAGE MY LIFE

WHAT ARE your non-negotiables for which, like Martin Luther, you will not recant? Evaluate whether your non-negotiables biblically reflect the heart of Jesus and make a list of them. Perhaps keep the list in your Bible or another familiar place to occasionally remind you.

THE DESIRE TO stand unashamed before his heavenly Father gave Luther strength to boldly proclaim God's truth. Everyone will one day stand before God. How does this truth shape the way you see others around you? And, how should it motivate your conversations?

FOR FURTHER REFLECTION & ENGAGEMENT

WHAT DID I learn from Martin Luther's life and story?

. . .

DID Martin's story stir something in me I need to pay attention to and talk to God about?

WHAT CLEAR, MEASURABLE "NEXT STEP" should I take in response to what God is showing me?

WHO IN THE Kingdom community will I ask to encourage me in this and keep me accountable?

WHY THIS LESSON, this day? What's God up to in deepening my faith and multiplying His Kingdom?

14

D.L. MOODY (1837-1899)

DECLARATION 14 – IT'S MY TURN TO SHARE THE GOOD NEWS OF JESUS WITH THE LOST

In 1855, Dwight (D.L.) Moody was a teenager with a life-ambition to earn a fortune. With only a fifth-grade education behind him, however, Dwight decided pursuing a job was a better plan. So, he moved to Boston to work in his uncle's shoe store. It was there that an everyday lover of God and people, Ed Kimbell, helped change the trajectory of Dwight's life by introducing him to Jesus. Knowing Jesus changed everything for Dwight! He committed the rest of his life to passionately spreading the gospel and influenced millions for God's Kingdom.

Ed Kimbell was an ordinary person, with an ordinary job, but an extraordinary love for God and others. He was also Dwight's Sunday School teacher. One day, Ed felt God prompting him to go to the shoe store where Dwight worked and share his faith story with Dwight. Ed hesitated at first, but God gave him the courage to go. Dwight was in the backroom stocking shoes. Ed shared his story and God's. Dwight responded!

Dwight never forgot the bold actions of this ordinary man who led him to a relationship with Jesus at his workplace. It compelled him to be bold in sharing his own faith with others. After all, he reasoned, if an ordinary man like Ed Kimball could be used in such ways to build God's Kingdom, so could he.

Dwight moved to Chicago and began his own ministry to children in the disadvantaged areas of the city. He would gather children from the streets and the docks around Chicago and tell them the stories of the Bible. Seeing the same authentic love for God and others which Ed Kimbell had demonstrated to Dwight, many of the children responded to the gospel.

Dwight pursued ordination as a pastor, but his limited formal education disqualified him. That would not deter Dwight. His Sunday School grew into a full-fledged church. Dwight became tireless in his efforts to reach people around him for Christ. He distributed tracts, held daily prayer meetings, and even helped evangelize Union troops during the Civil War. His methods were simple yet fruitful. He believed if your life and words attest to others that you genuinely love them, they will often believe how much God loves them too.

Two significant events motivated Dwight to share the gospel with as many people as possible as often as possible. One event happened in 1871 during an evangelistic service in Chicago. Dwight was preaching one evening on how God desired everyone to repent and be saved. Since it was a series of meetings on the subject, Dwight told them to return the next evening for an opportunity to respond to the gospel message. That night, the Great Chicago Fire broke out, and hundreds lost their lives—including many who had heard Dwight preach that evening. He was devastated, and he determined that he would never again miss a chance to compel people to respond immediately to the message of Christ.

The Great Chicago Fire destroyed Dwight's church, home, and the YMCA where he ministered. Seeking funds to rebuild the church, Dwight traveled to New York City. While there, he had another experience that profoundly shaped his ministry. As he walked down Wall Street, he felt "a presence and power" unlike anything he had ever experienced. The encounter was so powerful that he cried out, "Hold Lord, it is enough!" Dwight received fresh ministry purpose, vision, and power from the Holy Spirit that day. With fresh new passion ablaze in his heart for the "evangelization of the world in this generation," preaching the gospel became his number one priority.

When he returned to Chicago, even Dwight noticed a profound difference in his ministry. He reflected, my "sermons were no different, but now hundreds were being saved." At that point, he set a goal for himself. He determined that he was going to win someone to Christ every day for the rest of his life, God willing. He wrote the commitment down in his journal and promised to keep it "even if he didn't get any sleep at night."

And Dwight not only personally won people to Christ daily, he also established three Christian schools, a publishing business, a Christian conference, and a Bible institute. He inspired countless preachers to win souls through revival and continued doing so himself. In fact, he was still preaching six sermons a day just one month before he died!

It's reported Dwight traveled a million miles, preached to one hundred million people, and won a million souls to Christ. He chose to center his ministry in Chicago and focus it primarily on the most disadvantaged sections of the city, believing no one else would care to reach this part of the city's overlooked and undervalued population.

Dwight Moody, though ordinary in many ways, was compelled by an extraordinary passion and love for those spiritually lost. He won millions to Christ, establishing a profound soul-winning legacy. Dwight could never have imagined as a teenager how "rich" he would become, not in dollars and cents, but in the unsurpassable worth of knowing God, glorifying Him, and multiplying His Kingdom.

Dwight's Significant Contribution

Despite his lack of formal training, Dwight Moody did more to reach his generation for Christ than any other layperson. Through popularizing the Sunday School and pioneering many aspects of crusade evangelism, he personally introduced more than one million people to Christ. In addition, he founded Moody Bible Institute, one of the first and most well-known Bible colleges in the United States, thereby multiplying generations of future Kingdom laborers for worldwide impact.

Recommended Reading

D.L. Moody, The Greatest Evangelist of the Nineteenth Century, by Faith Coxe Bailey

A Passion for Souls: The Life of D.L. Moody, by Lyle W. Dorsett

Notable Quote

"If this world is going to be reached, I am convinced that it must be done by men and women of average talent. After all, there are comparatively few people in this world who have great talents."

IT'S MY TURN TO ...

ENGAGE THE STORY

Ed Kimbell obediently responded to God's prompting to share Jesus with Dwight at his workplace. He could have made excuses that he would see him in Sunday school. However, his boldness made an eternal impact on Dwight Moody. Do you regularly obey Jesus immediately? What difference have you seen in immediate obedience versus delayed obedience in your own life?

Do you have a hard time sharing your faith with others? Why or why not? Moody believed that if the world was going to be reached, it would come at the hand of men and women with average talent. How do Kimbell and Moody encourage you when it comes to sharing your faith, and overcoming any obstacles you might have?

ENGAGE GOD'S WORD

READ I JOHN 3:16-18. Dwight's methods of sharing the gospel were simple, yet effective. He believed that if you showed others genuine love by spoken truth and by action, then they would believe God loved them too. What could loving God and loving others look like for you this week?

Read Luke 8:26-40. How did the man set free from spiritual darkness do to tell others about Jesus? Did it seem overly complex? What has Jesus done to transform your life? What if you began to simply tell others the story of how Jesus has worked in your life?

ENGAGE MY LIFE

Write out your Jesus transformation story (This can be your salvation moment or another time when Jesus showed up for you). Keep it short enough to tell others in 1-2 minutes, structuring it in this way:

- What was your life like before Jesus transformed you? What felt need or difficulty did you face?

- What led to you encountering Jesus? Why did you go to Him? What did Jesus do?

- What was different in your life as a result?

- Put your story together and practice sharing it with another believer, so you will be ready to share with the lost!

List five people in your sphere of influence who do not know Jesus Christ. Make a commitment to pray for each of these people daily. You may be part of God's answer to your prayer, so set up a time to meet with them, and ask God to give you boldness to tell them your Jesus transformation story. After you share your story, ask them, "would you like to learn more about Jesus?" and see what God does!

FOR FURTHER REFLECTION & ENGAGEMENT

W︎HAT DID I learn from D.L. Moody's life and story?

D︎ID DWIGHT'S story stir something in me I need to pay attention to and talk to God about?

W︎HAT CLEAR, MEASURABLE "NEXT STEP" should I take in response to what God is showing me?

W︎HO IN THE Kingdom community will I ask to encourage me in this and keep me accountable?

W︎HY THIS LESSON, this day? What's God up to in deepening my faith and multiplying His Kingdom?

15

HUDSON TAYLOR (1832-1905)

DECLARATION 15 – IT'S MY TURN TO GO WHEREVER GOD SENDS ME

"A land of mystery and intrigue," the storyteller began, "well-known for silk, jade, and tea." Twelve-year old Hudson Taylor sat enthralled along with his siblings as his father, James, expounded on one of Hudson's favorite topics: China. A fascinating land indeed. It was also a country with great spiritual need and ripe with Kingdom harvest potential.

"Why are there only a half dozen Protestants working in that great land?" mused Hudson's father. Young Hudson chimed in, "When I am a man, I mean to be a missionary and go to China!" The thought was amusing for the Taylor family as they got up from the dinner table. Hudson was a sickly little child and the thought of him surviving the rigorous life of a missionary seemed like a farfetched dream, if not an impossibility altogether.

In the summer of 1849, Hudson was all alone reading a spiritual tract that pierced his heart with the truth of the gospel. His mother had been praying for him at the time of his conversion. She knew before he told her about his special encounter with God that the burden of sin had been rolled away.

As with many new believers, spiritual battle challenged his newfound relationship with Jesus. By December of that same year, the battle was intense. Hudson became obsessed with the fear he couldn't live up to his commitment to God. He was keenly aware of God's presence, but something wasn't right. Feelings of failure and unworthiness overwhelmed him. For Hudson, this was a life and death matter. Everything was at stake. He must settle the issues, whatever they may be, that kept him from total commitment to God's will for his life.

All alone, just as it was at his conversion, Hudson fell to his knees in prayer. He cried out to God. Hudson asked God for grace to keep him true. He pleaded for God to break the power of sin. He offered a fresh dedication of himself to God and promised to go anywhere and do anything God desired. Hudson surrendered his life unreservedly to God's will.

In that moment, God met Hudson with a profound assurance that his prayers had been answered. And with what seemed as clear as an audible voice, God spoke, "Then go for me to China!" From that moment, Hudson's mind was made up. Nothing could deter him from pursuing God's call so clearly given.

With calling comes preparation and provision. At age seventeen, Hudson had little idea what was needed to serve as a missionary to China. Even finding a book about China would prove challenging. But Hudson was determined. Someone gifted him with a copy of the writings of Luke in the Mandarin dialect. He began learning the Chinese language by painstakingly reading it. Within weeks his hard work and ingenuity had enabled him to decipher 500 Chinese words.

Hudson soon realized he didn't have to be on Chinese soil to be involved in ministry to China. He could pray and urge others to pray. He could financially support and encourage missionaries already on the ground or preparing to go. In his heart, however, Hudson was deeply burdened for the millions of Chinese people living beyond the port cities of China. They had no way of hearing the good news of the gospel. Someone had to tell them. More than ever, Hudson felt compelled to go.

Hudson learned of a book written about China from a Christian perspective. The Congregational minister in his town was said to have a copy. In early 1850 he went to borrow it, hoping to deepen his understanding of how to prepare for service in China. "Why do you want to read it?" asked the minister as he pulled the book from the shelf. Hudson explained his desire to go to China as a missionary. "And how do you propose to get there?" It was a question Hudson had not thought about in detail. He mumbled something about the disciples going out without means at the Lord's command. The minister replied, "Ah, my boy, as you grow older you will get wiser than that. Such an idea would do very well in the days when Christ himself was on earth, but not now."

Hudson read the book anyway. His resolve continued to deepen. In a letter to his sister Amelia he wrote, "Poor, neglected China! Scarcely anyone cares about it. And that immense country, containing nearly a fourth of the human race, is left in ignorance and darkness." Hudson, as determined as ever, traded his feather bed for a less accommodating sleeping surface to prepare himself for the rigors of life in the interior of China and redoubled his efforts to learn Chinese.

Three years later, on September 19, 1853, barely twenty-one years of age, Hudson boarded the freight ship Dumfries and headed to China as the ship's only passenger. The voyage lasted twenty-three weeks from Liverpool to Shanghai. It was a journey of faith that would last a lifetime. Hudson had surrendered his life to the will and call of God, a call to the people of China who had yet to hear the life-changing news of the gospel.

With enduring faith, Hudson dedicated his life to serve God in China. He suffered persecution and poverty. He endured numerous physical maladies. He trusted God and asked Him alone to supply all needs. Through tireless effort, determination, and constant prayer, Hudson Taylor began the China Inland Mission. His passion for the spiritually lost and his unwavering faith in Christ have seldom been equaled. His missionary ingenuity, unusual prayer life, and exemplary missionary service has lit the way for thousands to follow in his footsteps.

Hudson's Significant Contribution
Hudson Taylor initiated a new era of missionary activity by moving

beyond the coast lands and focusing on the untapped interior of China. Hudson's life of dependence on Jesus and practical faith not only led countless to Christ in China but empowered and multiplied innumerable others to join the mission, both in China and worldwide.

Recommended Reading
Hudson Taylor, by Hudson Taylor

Hudson Taylor's Spiritual Secret, by Dr. & Mrs. Howard Taylor

Notable Quote
"Our aim is not elaborate appeals for help, but rather to obtain successful laborers. First in earnest prayer to God to thrust forth laborers and second the deepening of the spiritual life of the church, so that men should be unable to stay at home."

IT'S MY TURN TO …

ENGAGE THE STORY

"Hudson was a sickly little child and the thought of him surviving the rigorous life of a missionary seemed like a farfetched dream, if not an impossibility altogether." Is there a dream, vision, or hope God has put in your heart that seems "farfetched"? What seems so impossible?

HUDSON WROTE, "Nor is God's work ever intended to be stationary, but always advancing." Has your Kingdom laboring been stagnant lately? Regarding God's mission, what ways have you been spiritually stuck or lazy? How can we better recognize when we're not "advancing" but are retreating or motionless?

ENGAGE GOD'S WORD

It's My Turn

READ ROMANS 9:1-3. Hudson was so burdened for the lost in China that he was "unable to stay at home." Like Hudson, have you ever experienced God's heart for a group of lost people so deeply, that it required action? Ask God what that might look like in your own life.

READ GENESIS 12:1-4 and Luke 10:2-3a. In addition to praying for laborers, are you willing to go yourself? Ask God which harvest fields He is calling you to engage. Is there a new place God is calling you into?

ENGAGE MY LIFE

HUDSON STRUGGLED EARLY on with issues that might hinder his total commitment to God. What did Hudson do with his feelings of inadequacies? What promises did he make to God? When it comes to God's worldwide mission, how do you feel inadequate? Talk to God about what it would look like for you to make an unreserved commitment to Him today.

PRAY AND ASK God to employ you in engaging unreached people groups (often called frontier or unengaged groups). Ask God specifically for who, what, where, when, and how He wants to use you. Commit to doing whatever God prompts you to do.

FOR FURTHER REFLECTION & ENGAGEMENT

WHAT DID I learn from Hudson Taylor's life and story?

DID Hudson's story stir something in me I need to pay attention to and talk to God about?

. . .

WHAT CLEAR, MEASURABLE "NEXT STEP" should I take in response to what God is showing me?

WHO IN THE Kingdom community will I ask to encourage me in this and keep me accountable?

WHY THIS LESSON, this day? What's God up to in deepening my faith and multiplying His Kingdom?

16

JARENA LEE (1783-1864)

DECLARATION 16 – IT'S MY TURN TO COURAGEOUSLY EMBRACE GOD'S CALLING

Jarena Lee was a Kingdom-advancing game-changer. She was the first woman authorized to preach in the African Methodist Episcopal Church and courageously blazed a trail for other women called by God to do the same.

Jarena, an African American, was born free in Cape May, New Jersey in 1783. Her family was quite poor, so her parents thought it best to send Jarena to work as a servant maid when she was seven-years old.

Jarena's childhood was troubling. The teachings she received made her feel unloved and unwanted as a "wretched sinner." She struggled with suicidal thoughts and fantasized about drowning herself on several occasions. God spared her. Through constant prayer and numerous conversations with God, she came to saving faith and the thoughts of ending her life ceased. Jarena came to realize these were Satan's attacks against God's plan for her life.

When Jarena was nineteen, she moved to Philadelphia and began attending Bethel African Methodist Episcopal (AME) Church pastored by Reverend Richard Allen. She felt at home there. It became the place God would use to work out her calling and His Kingdom plans.

On one occasion of solitude, Jarena heard a distinct voice she believed was the Lord's. "Go and preach the gospel," she heard Him say. She replied out loud, "No one will believe me." Again, the voice rang out, "Preach the gospel; I will put words in your mouth, and you will turn your enemies to become your friends."

Jarena shared the news with Reverend Allen that God had spoken to her and commanded her to preach. Reverend Allen believed her but sadly informed her that church law made no provision for women preachers. Jarena did not want to be subversive to the church, neither could she deny what God had spoken. "If the man may preach, because the Savior died for him," she postulated, "why not the woman, seeing he died for her also? Is he not a whole Savior, instead of half of one?"

Jarena was free from human slavery, but she felt enslaved in her mind: a call to preach, with no means to accomplish it. Still, she refused to cause disruption in the church. She obediently waited on the Holy Spirit's movement. She held prayer meetings in her home, exhorted her brothers and sisters, and reminded them that they were God's chosen people.

Jarena held to God's call and promise for the next eight years. During that time, she married Joseph Lee, himself a pastor. Joseph and Jarena had two children, and they continued to serve the Lord faithfully. Jarena suffered a near-death illness. The Lord once again spared her. Her husband too became ill. Unfortunately, he did not survive. Jarena was widowed with two children after six years of marriage.

In 1817, during a Sunday service at the Bethel Church, the preacher for the day began to fumble his words and lose his way. He stood awkwardly silent. Jarena sensed God was making room for her to publicly use her gift. The sermon that the suddenly-muted speaker had begun to preach was on Jonah 2, "Salvation is of the Lord." Jarena stood and began, "I am this Jonah. I am like him, because he was called to preach to Nineveh and didn't want to go. I am reluctant as well." Jarena passionately poured out her heart and preached for 45 minutes. Reverend Allen, who had become "Bishop" Allen since their initial calling conversation, was in attendance. Bishop Allen affirmed Jarena, "You are called to preach!"

While Jarena's message was powerful and God's Word had been

accurately proclaimed, a woman preacher was difficult for people to accept. Jarena received a lot of critique, even from women who knew her consistent character and authenticity of faith. When asked why she thought it was okay that a woman preached, she responded, "Did not Mary preach the risen Savior, and is not the doctrine of the resurrection the very climax of Christianity? Then did Mary, a woman, preach the gospel? for she preached the resurrection of the crucified son of God." In that very moment, Jarena later said, "I believe the Holy Ghost made room for me."

Over the remainder of Jarena's life, her preaching was received with mixed reaction: some accepted her, others did not. She did not let the opinions of others sway nor deter her. Her calling was from God.

Jarena's call was clear, her heart and mind resolute. What people thought of her did not matter. What God thought of her did. That's why she became an itinerant minister. Her work required great sacrifice—from finding someone to care for her children while she was away, to earning money as a seamstress to pay the bills. Jarena traveled mile upon mile on foot, horseback, and by boat in order to share the good news of Jesus. One year alone, she traveled 2,300 miles and preached 178 sermons. Why? In her words, "because I love God."

Jarena Lee died penniless in Philadelphia sometime in early 1864. Despite her inauspicious end, Jarena's courage to heed God's call, crossing barriers of race, gender, and dogma for the sake of the Kingdom continues to inspire and encourage fellow laborers today. "I set the trail ablaze, my brothers and sisters," Jarena once said, "not just for myself, but for those of you following behind. And I set it ablaze so that you will also answer the call on your life and say, 'Lord, here I am.'"

Jarena's Significant Contribution

Jarena's heart was deeply stirred as she heard a clear call from God to "go and preach the gospel." She remained humble and poised to move at God's pace, courageously trusting in God to make a way in the face of obstacles and barriers. In a day when most African Americans and most women were not able to freely travel and proclaim the gospel, Jarena walked by faith. In God's timing and by His provision, Jarena crossed barriers of race, gender, and dogma; and by doing so, set forth an inspiring example for all to courageously embrace God's calling and proclaim the gospel, without reservation.

Recommended Reading
Religious Experience and Journal of Mrs. Jarena Lee, by Jarena Lee.

Doers of the Word: African American Women Speakers and Writers in the North (1830–1880), by Carla Peterson.

Notable Quote
"I felt as if aided from above. My tongue was cut loose, the stammerer spoke freely; the love of God, and of his service, burned with a vehement flame within me—his name was glorified among the people."

IT'S MY TURN TO ...

ENGAGE THE STORY

Jarena believed God had called her to preach, even when she was informed that her church didn't allow this role for women. It took eight years from the time Jarena received God's call before the Holy Spirit opened a door of opportunity for her. Yet Jarena chose to trust God and His timing. How do you see evidence of this in her story? How did Jarena spend that time training for her calling?

JARENA COURAGEOUSLY CROSSED barriers for sake of her calling to preach the gospel. What kind of struggles and opposition do you think she faced? How do you think she pressed forward and endured?

ENGAGE GOD'S WORD

It's My Turn

READ JOSHUA 1:7-9. What instructions did God give Joshua to sustain him as he stepped into his calling? What promise did God make to him? These truths applied to Jarena and they apply to us as well.

READ I CORINTHIANS 4:1-5. Jarena believed in the call God had given her and made up her mind to obey. She cared more about what God thought of her than what others thought of her. Ask God if there are any areas in your life where the opinions of others have kept your from embracing His calling for your life.

ENGAGE MY LIFE

ONE YEAR ALONE, Jarena traveled 2,300 miles and preached 178 sermons, "because she loved God." Jarena put feet to her love for God. Ask God how you might "put feet" to your love for Him this week. Then, commit to it.

JARENA SAID OF HER PREACHING, "I believe the Holy Ghost made room for me." Up until that point, Jarena chose to move at God's pace, waiting for the moment that He would make a way. Is the Holy Spirit "making room" or preparing a Kingdom assignment for you? Dare to ask. As you wait for God's timing, are you preparing and listening, like Jarena, so that you are ready the very moment God opens a door of opportunity? What could that look like for you?

FOR FURTHER REFLECTION & ENGAGEMENT

WHAT DID I learn from Jarena Lee's life and story?

. . .

Did Jarena's story stir something in me I need to pay attention to and talk to God about?

What clear, measurable "next step" should I take in response to what God is showing me?

Who in the Kingdom community will I ask to encourage me in this and keep me accountable?

Why this lesson, this day? What's God up to in deepening my faith and multiplying His Kingdom?

17

JOHN PATON (1824-1907)

DECLARATION 17 – IT'S MY TURN TO BECOME A THREAT TO THE KINGDOM OF DARKNESS

John Paton, the eldest of eleven children, was born in Scotland. His father was a stocking manufacturer, and from the age of twelve John began working and learning his father's trade. The fourteen-hour days were difficult, but all hands were needed to maintain the family's humble, three-room thatched cottage.

John learned a lot about life, work, and faith in those early years. John was greatly influenced by the devoutness of his father, who went to his "prayer closet" three times a day and called the family to gather for prayer every morning and evening. It was in these formative years of his youth that John felt called by God to serve overseas as a missionary.

In his late teens, John moved forty miles away to Glasgow where he studied theology and medicine. He also ministered among the poor in a degraded section of the city. Balancing school, work, and ministry was difficult. John had to suspend his studies several times in order to raise money for school. But God didn't waste his time. John's odd jobs of distributing tracts and teaching school along with his work among the poor all contributed to the many skills and fortitude needed in sharing the gospel as a missionary.

In 1858, John and his wife, Mary, arrived on the island of Tanna, located northeast of Australia in the southern portion of The New Hebrides Islands. The Paton's arrival marked a significant step in fulfilling the call God placed on John's life so many years prior. It was a great day to celebrate, but the journey ahead would significantly test John's faith.

The Tanna natives were a barbaric, cannibalistic people who practiced sorcery and witchcraft. The task of establishing a missionary work among them was daunting. John was not the first to attempt to bring the gospel to Tanna. Several other missionaries had preceded him and had been killed or run off the island, a history the natives were quite proud of!

In the first few months after arriving, tragedy struck. John's wife and newborn son died of malaria. John buried them together, close to their house in Resolution Bay. He spent nights sleeping on their grave to protect them from the local cannibals. John himself was afflicted with malaria and battled the disease on fourteen different occasions in his first few years.

John's struggles were not only physical and familial, they were also spiritual. The initial curiosity of the Tanna people quickly gave way to hatred and fear as John began to teach against their beliefs and proclaim Jehovah as the only true God. John would often be surrounded by musket or hatchet-toting natives intent on killing him as he worked.

Among John's greatest opposition were the Sacred Men. They were the spiritual leaders of Tanna, who claimed to control life and death, sickness and rain. Their practices included dances, rituals, and sacrifices to their god, Nahak. They often conducted their sorcery through ritualizing a piece of eaten food they obtained from the individual they were cursing.

One Sunday, three of the Sacred Men called John out and proclaimed they could kill him. John determined with the Lord to put them to the test. Giving each of them a piece of fruit of which he had eaten, he challenged them to kill him without the help of muskets, arrows or other weapons, but only through the power of their god, Nahak. The Sacred Men immediately wrapped the fruit in the leaves of a sacred tree and created candle-like bundles to burn. Lighting a fire, they began to slowly burn the candles. They danced, chanted incantations, and began wildly waving the candles.

In terror, the natives all fled. John, however, stayed. The efforts of Nahak and the Sacred Men were futile. Exhausted, the three Sacred Men decided to quit for the day. Calling together all the Sacred Men on Tanna, they determined to kill John and promised it would be accomplished within a week.

John began to pray against the Sacred Men and their power. He asked God to protect him so that the Tanna people might see that Jehovah, not Nahak, was the one, true God. Throughout the week, the Sacred Men sent scouts to inquire about John's condition. Each time, the Sacred Men were disappointed with the report of John's vitality.

A week had passed, and John returned to the village in perfect health. The Sacred Men admitted to the people that their attempts to kill John by the powers of Nahak had failed. John's God was stronger and had protected him. The Tanna people were in awe of Jehovah and His power.

That was one of many spiritual battles John encountered on Tanna. The islanders were a fearful people often swayed by the speeches of their leaders and Sacred Men who wished John harm. After four years on the island of Tanna, John was forced to flee. In time, word traveled to John that the Tanna people were begging for his return. They wanted to learn more about his God.

John returned to share God's story and how they could be a part of the story as well. In time, the people of Tanna embraced the gospel. Confidence in God and the power of prayer allowed John, and later others, to overcome the dark forces at work on Tanna.

John remarried, and he and his wife continued to minister to people throughout the region. By 1899, the entire island of Aniwa, the island closest to Tanna, proclaimed faith in Jesus Christ. When John's faithful work was done, missionaries were on the ground in twenty-five of the thirty New Hebrides islands. John discovered both difficulty and utter joy in trusting God through all circumstances and overcoming spiritual darkness with the light of Christ.

John's Significant Contribution
John Paton reminds us that it is right to endure hardship, suffer, and risk death in the process of obedience to God's call. John's life reveals that those who keep up their spiritual fervor, die to themselves, and live for Christ will threaten the Kingdom of darkness!

Recommended Reading
John G. Paton, Hero of the South Seas, by Bessie G. Byrum

Missionary Patriarch: The True Story of John G. Paton, by John G. Paton

Notable Quote
"Life, any life, would be well spent, under any conceivable conditions in bringing one human soul to know and love and serve God and His Son… That fame will prove immortal, when all the poems and pyramids of earth have gone to dust."

IT'S MY TURN TO …

ENGAGE THE STORY

John faced immense hardships trying to reach a cannibalistic tribe: losing his wife and child, sickness, being threatened with weapons, constant danger, seemingly unresponsive people etc. John could only forge forward through complete dependence upon God. What kind of example did John's father set that built a foundation of godly dependence?

OTHER MISSIONARIES HAD GONE before John and either were killed or fled. With all the opposition John faced, no one would have faulted him for leaving. Yet John considered infiltrating the darkness more important than his safety. Do you value personal safety and comfort more than shining Jesus into the darkness? What would it

It's My Turn

look like for you to focus on shining the light of Christ and to trust God to take care of your life? What might happen if you did?

ENGAGE GOD'S WORD

READ 1 KINGS 18:20-40. John challenged the Sacred Men and their false god, Nahak, in the same way Elijah challenged the prophets of Baal. What do we learn about God's power over spiritual darkness from John's life and from the story of Elijah? (see Hebrews 13:8). How might knowing God's Word encourage us to boldly threaten the kingdom of darkness?

READ EPHESIANS 6:10-20. Who is our true enemy? John understood that he was fighting a spiritual battle, not against people but for people, against "the spiritual forces of evil in the heavenly places." Look back at each piece of armor. What does each piece of armor stand for? How do you see that John was equipped with the armor of God in his life? Are you putting on the full armor of God in your life?

ENGAGE MY LIFE

JOHN DEALT with spiritual darkness and warfare constantly. It is easy to forget that our struggle is against "spiritual forces." How has God's Word and John's story given you a fresh perspective when it comes to facing our enemy?

WE OFTEN PRAISE independence and self-sustainability. John's practice of prayer and complete dependence upon God brought victory over the kingdom of darkness in a way that other men had failed to do. Moving forward, how will you begin to effectively battle on your knees for those trapped in the kingdom of darkness?

FOR FURTHER REFLECTION & ENGAGEMENT

What did I learn from John Paton's life and story?

Did John's story stir something in me I need to pay attention to and talk to God about?

What clear, measurable "next step" should I take in response to what God is showing me?

Who in the Kingdom community will I ask to encourage me in this and keep me accountable?

Why this lesson, this day? What's God up to in deepening my faith and multiplying His Kingdom?

18

WILLIAM BOOTH (1829-1912)

DECLARATION 18 – IT'S MY TURN TO LOVE THE OVERLOOKED AND UNDERVALUED

Before William Booth became a full-time minister, he conducted services in small, rural settings as a lay preacher. Even as a teenager, his heart for the economically disadvantaged and pushed aside was evident. When he received his local preacher's license in the Methodist church, his superintendent asked him to settle for a more "regular" ministry role as a local church pastor rather than the hard labor of working with the poor. His doctor advised against it as well, telling William that his health was so poor that he was totally unfit for the strain of the preacher's life. William humbly replied, "Unfit? Of course, I am unfit in myself. But in the strength God gives me, I am going to do the thing God has called me to do."

That doctor had no way of knowing that the strenuous labor required working among London's impoverished people would make a minister's life seem posh in comparison. Nor did the doctor have any way of knowing that William would live to be eighty-three and launch a worldwide, renown organization called The Salvation Army that would bring life and wholeness to millions for nearly a century and a half and counting.

William's success with The Salvation Army didn't come without trial and hardship. The first thirty years, the ministry faced ongoing funding needs and clashes with groups that opposed The Army's marches against alcohol. In 1882 alone, 662 Salvation Army soldiers (workers) were assaulted. Opposition also arose from the press and The Church of England. William's work was squeezed on every side.

But William, the Army's general, lived to see the day when the troops would be honored around the world. England's own King Edward VII did just that at Buckingham Palace in 1904. When the king asked William to sign his autograph album, he summarized his life's work as he wrote:

Your Majesty,
  Some men's ambition is art,
  Some men's ambition is fame,
  Some men's ambition is gold,
  My ambition is the souls of men.

William's wife, Catherine, shared his same ambition for spiritually lost people, especially those unwanted and unloved. As a young girl, Catherine watched as a constable escorted a criminal down the street to prison to the chants of an angry mob. Catherine perceived that the convict didn't have a friend in the world, especially in that moment. His loneliness struck her. Determined that he should know there was at least one soul that cared about him, Catherine darted to his side and trudged down the street with him. No wonder The Salvation Army had such great Kingdom fruitfulness. William and Catherine were motivated by God's great compassion, which they modeled daily.

In addition to serving the physically sustaining needs of the overlooked and undervalued, the Salvation Army team was determined to be the church beyond walls and steeples. They began holding "street meetings" on downtown corners. Assembling a brass band, complete with tambourines, drums, and talented singers, people of all ages and

It's My Turn

walks of life gathered to be entertained. Once gathered, the gospel was powerfully shared. Many responded and the Kingdom was advanced by meeting people in creative ways "right where they were."

A contemporary writer in William's day once compared two people. The first was a woman who died in London. She was famous and known as "the best dressed woman in Europe." While she bequeathed almost a thousand frocks after her death, each one given reflected a life with "the same unseeing eyes, the same deaf ears, and the same enameled, painted face."

The second person the author described was a man who also died in London. He was a man who owned, not a thousand frocks, but one suit; its color blue, its collar red. The man had but one uniform, but he lived a thousand lives. His name was William Booth.

Dr. J. Wilbur Chapman, an American evangelist who also composed the hymn, Jesus! What A Friend for Sinners, once visited William in London near the end of William's life. After listening to stories of his trials, conflicts, and victories, Chapman asked William if he would disclose the secret for his success. "He hesitated for a second," Chapman said, "and I saw tears come into his eyes and steal down his cheeks. 'I will tell you the secret. God has had all there was of me. There have been men with greater brains than I, men with greater opportunities; but from the day I got the poor of London on my heart and a vision of what Jesus Christ could do, I made up my mind that God would have all of William Booth there was.'" Dr. Chapman said he went away from the meeting knowing "that the greatness of a man's power is the measure of his surrender."

Just before his death, William appeared a final time to speak. His health was failing, and he only had sight in one eye. To an audience of over four thousand, he spoke for an hour and a half. "I want to do more for humanity," he said, "and I want to do a great deal more for Jesus. There are thousands of poor, wretched, suffering and sinning people crying out to us for help, and I want to do something for them!"

Well over a hundred years and counting since William's death, the vision-driven Kingdom work of faith, care, and perseverance God began with William continues. "I want a life spent in putting other people right," William once declared. God's faithfulness continues to honor William's life-giving aspiration.

William's Significant Contribution

William Booth began a movement that changed the way his nation viewed and addressed the poor. Because of his relentless efforts among poverty-stricken people, the Salvation Army now has branches worldwide. It is still touching lives today with generosity and compassion, offering hope, and teaching the gospel. The Salvation Army has affected innumerable lives for Christ as a result of William's vision.

Recommended Reading

William Booth, Founder of the Salvation Army, by Harold Begbie

Notable Quote

"I want a life spent in putting other people right."

IT'S MY TURN TO …

ENGAGE THE STORY

William's life was full of taking risks. He risked is health, finances, reputation, and safety. Meeting the needs of the poor, meant going to the places most people were not willing to go. What kind of explanations are given in this story to explain William's daring actions?

William told the king, "My ambition is the souls of men." Take a few moments to reflect on your life up to this point. What would you say has been your life's ambition thus far?

ENGAGE GOD'S WORD

It's My Turn

READ ISAIAH 58:6-10. What does this passage tell us about God's heart and our responsibility as His people?

GOD HAD PRESSED an incredible burden on William's heart for the overlooked, undervalued, suffering, and sinful people of London. Read Luke 14:11-24. Clearly, William had been given God's vision and heart. What is the master's vision for his house? How well does your life reflect that vision?

ENGAGE MY LIFE

WILLIAM SAID, "I made up my mind that God would have all of William Booth there was." Chapman concluded, "that the greatness of a man's power is the measure of his surrender." How much have you surrendered to God? Ask Him if there are any parts of your life that you have not been willing to let go of?

THE OFFICERS IN WILLIAM'S "ARMY" promised, "For Christ's sake, to feed the poor, clothe the naked, love the unlovable, and befriend the friendless." If possible, visit a Salvation Army or other ministry in your area that serves the homeless, poor, and downtrodden. Take a tour, ask questions, and volunteer. Ask God to break your heart for what breaks His, and to see others as He does.

FOR FURTHER REFLECTION & ENGAGEMENT

WHAT DID I learn from William Booth's life and story?

DID William's story stir something in me I need to pay attention to and talk to God about?

FORGE

. . .

WHAT CLEAR, MEASURABLE "NEXT STEP" should I take in response to what God is showing me?

WHO IN THE Kingdom community will I ask to encourage me in this and keep me accountable?

WHY THIS LESSON, this day? What's God up to in deepening my faith and multiplying His Kingdom?

19

WILLIAM CAREY (1761-1834)

DECLARATION 19 – IT'S MY TURN TO ENGAGE THE NATIONS

As a young man, William Carey studied geography on a homemade globe and noted the neglected countries of the world. He prayed God would make a way for him to help the "heathen nations" living in spiritual darkness. Reading Journal of Captain Cook's Last Voyage, which chronicled the adventures of a British sea captain in the South Pacific, young William was stirred toward missions. So profound was his stirring that his sister later noted she never heard William pray without including the unreached nations. To William, the unreached people in far-off lands weren't just statistics. They were people in need of the good news Jesus offers.

William had no qualifications to be a missionary except an undeniable conviction that God had called him to "the conversion of the heathens," to those who had never heard of Jesus. In 1786, he was ordained as a preacher at age twenty-five. Although he poured himself into local church ministry, his dreams of reaching out to faraway lands never left him.

William's combined brilliant intellect and spiritual passion for reaching the unreached were evident. When it came to the world beyond the local geography, William's training and experience often rose above that of his peers. Once while attending a ministers' meeting, a question was posed about an island in the East Indies. No one knew anything about the place. After plenty of time had been given for others to respond, William modestly rose to his feet and gave the location of the island and information he had gleaned about the spiritual condition of its people.

In his first year of pastoring, William was invited to participate in the Ministers' Fraternal of the Northampton Association. At one of the gatherings, William was asked to pose a question that would form the basis of the group's discussion for the day. He proposed they consider "Whether the command given to the apostles to teach all nations was not binding on all succeeding ministers to the end of the world, seeing that the accompanying promise was of equal extent."

His suggestion was harshly rebuked by the group's chairman. "Young man, sit down!" the chairman exclaimed. "When God pleases to convert the heathen, He will do it without your aid or mine." William was publicly humiliated and called a "miserable enthusiast." His peers, who saw his ideas as crazy and farfetched, lent him no support or encouragement.

The passion and genius William possessed was well hidden beneath his rustic exterior. He was short, often poorly dressed, wore an ill-fitted wig made of horsehair to cover his premature baldness, and had hands that were cracked and stained from years of working with leather as a shoemaker. On the surface, William had more than enough reasons to abort the mission God had chiseled on his heart. But he did not give up. He couldn't abandon the mission God had given him.

Two years into pastoring, William met Thomas Potts, a local businessman with a heart for missions. Potts implored William to put his ideas on evangelism in print. When William hedged on the idea, Potts contributed ten pounds toward the printing of a pamphlet exhorting Christians to accept responsibility for sharing the gospel with unreached nations.

William accepted the challenge and drew upon his eight years of research to write an eighty-seven-page booklet entitled, An Enquiry into the Obligation of Christians to Use Means for the Conversion of the Heathen. In this booklet, William poured out his soul. He carefully documented the geographic, cultural, and spiritual conditions of every known part of the world. From the early years of his childhood, God had been preparing William for this moment of destiny. Years of study, research, and prayer were coming to fruition.

The influence of William's booklet opened the door for him to speak before the Northamptonshire Baptist Association, a gathering of several local churches for mutual support and service. William preached from Isaiah 54:2-3, "Enlarge the place of thy tent... thy seed shall inhabit the Gentiles" (KJV). He summed up his fiery challenge to reach out to heathen nations with these words, "Expect great things from God. Attempt great things for God."

On October 2, 1792, a resolution was adopted creating the first Protestant mission agency. The first era of Protestant missions had begun.

After some years of discernment, William became a missionary to India. His strategy in India was threefold: preach the gospel, translate the Bible, and open schools. God accomplished all three through William. The first Hindu believer was baptized in 1800, and many more baptisms followed. William promoted literacy and education throughout the country and was responsible for translating the Bible into eleven languages.

William Carey, widely known as "The Father of Modern Missions," spent more than forty years as a missionary in India. His influence was great. His ministry was fruitful. He was a pioneer of faith. Still, his desire was to glorify God in all things. "When I am gone," he said on his deathbed, "say nothing about Dr. Carey. Speak only of Dr. Carey's Savior."

William's Significant Contribution
Because of his public stand for missions among pastors in England and his pioneer missionary efforts in India, William Carey is known as the "Father of Modern Missions." His urgency for the unreached, recognition of the need for contextualization, and respect for the national culture provided a lasting model for missionaries today.

Recommended Reading
William Carey, by Basil Miller

Notable Quote
"Expect great things from God. Attempt great things for God."

IT'S MY TURN TO …

ENGAGE THE STORY

William believed that all Christians should have a role in reaching the nations. While we might not agree with the chairman's declaration, "When God pleases to convert the heathen, He will do it without your aid or mine," is it possible that we believe, God will simply send someone else? Have you ever considered somehow becoming a part of mission efforts to reaching the nations? Prayerfully consider what your role should be in engaging the nations.

WILLIAM PRAYED that God would give him a chance to reach people across the world living in spiritual darkness. To him they weren't just statistics. "They were people in need of the good news Jesus offers." How might researching unreached people groups and consistently praying for them change your heart toward the spiritual condition of the world?

ENGAGE GOD'S WORD

READ MATTHEW 28:18-20 and Revelation 7:9-10. What does Revelation tell us heaven will look like? Knowing that there are still people groups that have not been reached with the good news of Jesus, what should your response be to the command given in Matthew?

. . .

It's My Turn

READ ROMANS 10:13-15; Psalm 96:1-3, 10; Acts 20:26-27; and Acts 1:8. Who is responsible for the proclamation of Jesus' message to the unreached among the nations? William challenged others to embrace God's heart for all nations and said, "Expect great things from God. Attempt great things for God." For any area where we feel inexperienced or lacking, where does our power come from? What does it enable us to do?

ENGAGE MY LIFE

OFTEN WHAT YOU PRAY FOR, where you spend your money, and how you invest your time can indicate your priorities. In your own life, what do these things say about your heart for the unreached world? On a scale of 1-10, assess your level of interest and concern for the unreached. Why did you choose the number you did? How could you increase your passion to see God's heart for all nations fully embraced?

WILLIAM ONCE WROTE, "We must plan and plod as well as pray." What unique gifts and skills can you use to advance the Kingdom in the nations you're praying for? Visit JoshuaProject.net to discover where unreached people groups exist. Choose several to pray for today. Then, begin researching what organizations are working to engage those groups, and ask God how you might partner with them. As it has been said, you can either "go, send, or disobey!"

FOR FURTHER REFLECTION & ENGAGEMENT

WHAT DID I learn from William Carey's life and story?

. . .

Did William's story stir something in me I need to pay attention to and talk to God about?

What clear, measurable "next step" should I take in response to what God is showing me?

Who in the Kingdom community will I ask to encourage me in this and keep me accountable?

Why this lesson, this day? What's God up to in deepening my faith and multiplying His Kingdom?

20

DAWSON TROTMAN (1906-1956)

DECLARATION 20 – IT'S MY TURN TO PRODUCE AND
MULTIPLY MORE KINGDOM LABORERS

Dawson "Daws" Trotman lived a rebellious lifestyle in high school. Gambling, drinking, stealing, and recklessness marked his days. Growing up in Arizona, Daws said and did many of the right Christian things, but it wasn't until he was twenty that Dawson fully committed his life to Christ. As with everything else in his life, if Daws was going to do something, he was going to do it 100%. He began living boldly for Christ and sharing the gospel with his friends. Dawson's life purpose became clear: he wanted to know Christ and make Christ known to every person he encountered.

Soon Dawson joined the Fishermen Club, a group that focused on evangelism and Bible study. Daws would often pray, "Lord, we're just reporting for duty. We don't know who we'll meet today or what their need will be; but give us the right word for them."

As Dawson had the opportunity to lead more and more people to Christ, he began to see the difference between winning souls and making disciples, between adding believers and reproducing Kingdom multipliers. Dawson began to shift his ministry focus. He began to feel a deep responsibility for discipling whoever he helped lead to Christ. No longer could he evangelize without discipling. "Don't bring spiritual babes to birth and leave them to die for lack of nourishment," he warned his fellow Kingdom laborers. Dawson had a growing conviction that person-to-person discipleship would multiply God's Kingdom far more effectively than any large group or large-scale impersonal approach.

In 1933, Dawson moved to San Diego to lead a ministry to sailors on Navy ships. That's where Dawson got closely connected with Les Spencer, a serviceman on the U.S.S. West Virginia. For several months, Dawson spent up-close time with Les, teaching him the Scriptures and what it meant to follow Jesus unreservedly.

Les got increasingly excited about what he was learning from Dawson. He wanted one of his shipmates to glean from it too. So, he asked Dawson if his friend could join them. Dawson's response surprised Les. "Absolutely not! You teach him," he said. "If your friend is going to be discipled, it will have to be you who does it." Les protested. He felt ill-equipped for the task. Dawson responded, "Doesn't matter. If you can't teach him what I've taught you, I've failed."

Les discipled his friend. His friend discipled another friend. Soon, the first Service Men's Bible Club was born. Dawson began meeting with Les and three other sailors. Before long, the original four servicemen were bringing their shipmates to Christ and discipling them. Again and again it repeated. A sailor would come to know Christ and then share Christ with another sailor. The gospel spread quickly, and God's Kingdom was multiplying.

By 1934, the group had grown so large that The Navigators: A Bible Club for Service Men was formed. The U.S.S. West Virginia eventually had Bible classes nearly every night and was nicknamed "The Floating Seminary!" In 1941, the world became The Navigators' parish. Servicemen, who had been discipled through the work Dawson started, were deployed around the world as the United States entered World War II.

Dawson continued the ministry of The Navigators. His bold challenge remained strong: multiply disciples, don't just add believers. In

It's My Turn

order for all people to be reached with the gospel, Dawson believed Christians needed to be about the business of "producing reproducers." Dawson would often ask believers, "Who, because of you, is carrying on the gospel of Christ?"

Spiritual multiplication, Dawson said, is "reaching the greatest number of people in the most effective way in the shortest possible time." Dawson believed that making and multiplying disciples was the best way to fulfill the Great Commission in a single generation.

Dawson Trotman died at age fifty in a drowning accident while helping a girl struggling in the water. In saving her life, he lost his own. To the very end, Dawson gave all he had so that others could experience the fullness of all God has for them.

The Navigators continues today to carry out the faithful work Dawson began. A ministry with a worldwide reach, The Navigators continues to use one-on-one relationships and small group discipleship to produce Kingdom reproducers and to bring to fruition Dawson's life motto: "To know Christ and make Him known."

Dawson's Significant Contribution

Dawson Trotman reintroduced the Church to the lost priority of relational disciple-making and spiritual multiplication. Today, the ministry he started is active around the world on college campuses, military bases, inner cities, prisons, and youth camps. The Navigators continue to disciple people "to follow Christ passionately by applying the Bible to their daily lives, passing on what they learn, and training new believers to reach others."

Recommended Reading

DAWS: The Story of Dawson Trotman, Founder of the Navigators, by Betty Lee Skinner

Notable Quote

"Oh Lord, help me build men, strong, holy, prepared men to go to the four corners of the world who will do the same."

IT'S MY TURN TO ...

ENGAGE THE STORY

Dawson would often pray, "Lord, we're just reporting for duty. We don't know who we'll meet today or what their need will be; but give us the right word for them." He trusted God to give him the words; his job was to just show up and be willing to share. Consider offering yourself to God in the same manner this week, looking for Kingdom opportunities.

THE CONCEPT of spiritual multiplication is based on the idea that more time with fewer people can have a more powerful and lasting impact than less time with more people. How could this method "reach the greatest number of people...in the shortest amount of time" as Dawson believed?

ENGAGE GOD'S WORD

JESUS PREACHED TO THE MASSES, but he spent up close, personal time with the twelve disciples. Read Mark 1:17 and Acts 1:8. What was the purpose of the personal training Jesus gave his disciples?

READ 2 TIMOTHY 2:2. Dawson believed that if those he discipled could not teach what they had been taught, then he had failed. Effective discipleship should be "producing reproducers." Who have you seen do this really well? How did they do it? Are you currently practicing this yourself?

ENGAGE MY LIFE

It's My Turn

Dawson's motto was "To know Christ, and to make Him known." The more we grow to know God, the more we'll long to share what we've learned and make Him known. Dawson would often ask, "Who, because of you, is carrying on the gospel of Christ?" Ask yourself this question and talk to God about what this is meant to look like in your life.

The process of spiritual multiplication is not complete until the laborers you reproduce are also reproducing more laborers. If you are currently discipling someone, what steps can you take to encourage him or her to disciple others?

If you are currently being discipled by someone, prayerfully consider who you might need to begin investing in. Forge has tools to help you to disciple others in practical ways (ForgeForward.org/Resources).

FOR FURTHER REFLECTION & ENGAGEMENT

What did I learn from Dawson Trotman's life and story?

Did Dawson's story stir something in me I need to pay attention to and talk to God about?

What clear, measurable "next step" should I take in response to what God is showing me?

Who in the Kingdom community will I ask to encourage me in this and keep me accountable?

. . .

Why this lesson, this day? What's God up to in deepening my faith and multiplying His Kingdom?

THE LABORERS DECLARATION

Like a runner in the relay race of human history, I accept the baton of responsibility to reach my generation for Christ. I cannot live for today, thinking only of myself. I cannot pretend that the unreached are not lost, that hell is not real, or that I am not accountable for the needs around me.

Laborers from other generations have gone before me. They have taken their turn at using their gifts to build God's Kingdom. Today, I commit myself to join their ranks as a laborer in my generation, seeking to cultivate the Christ-like characteristics and actions they displayed. It's my turn…

1. I affirm that intimacy with God is the foundation for all service to Him. It's my turn to love God with passion and intentionality.
2. I affirm that the character of Jesus is expressed to the world through unconditional love and sacrifice. It's my turn to sacrificially lay down my life for God and others.
3. I affirm that loving others requires a servant's heart. It's my turn to love and serve with humility.
4. I affirm that being a laborer will require a complete

The Laborers Declaration

surrender to the lordship of Christ. It's my turn to say yes to God with reckless abandon.

5. I affirm that God is bigger than any impossibilities that come my way. It's my turn to trust Jesus for a God-sized vision.
6. I affirm that God has designed a lifestyle for me that requires I depend on Him daily for His supernatural power. It's my turn to live by radical faith.
7. I affirm that being a living sacrifice brings persecution from others. It's my turn to willingly suffer for the Kingdom of God.
8. I affirm that we gain our lives only when we give them away, living to exalt God and not ourselves. It's my turn to die to self in order to exalt Christ.
9. I affirm the priority of prayer as the driving force behind all Kingdom advancement. It's my turn to intercede in prayer for the spiritually lost.
10. I affirm that a life lived with Christ requires endurance to finish strong. It's my turn to persevere in life and love.
11. I affirm that God most often uses ordinary people who are committed to Him in advancing His Kingdom. It's my turn to embrace my unique role in God's Kingdom.
12. I affirm that I am accountable for everything God has given me. It's my turn to use my God-given gifts for His glory.
13. I affirm that the Word of God is my final authority, and that I must stand for truth when the values of my culture contradict the values of God's Kingdom. It's my turn to stand for God's truth.
14. I affirm that only through Jesus can we have relationship with God and hope for eternity. It's my turn to share the good news of Jesus with the lost.
15. I affirm that as a Kingdom laborer I serve at the pleasure of King Jesus. It's my turn to go wherever God sends me.
16. I affirm that when God calls opposition and barriers will arise. It's my turn to courageously embrace God's calling.

17. I affirm that advancing God's Kingdom comes with spiritual resistance. It's my turn to become a threat to the kingdom of darkness.
18. I affirm that God cares for all people and sees the needs of the least, last, and lost. It's my turn to love the overlooked and undervalued.
19. I affirm God's purpose to establish His Kingdom among all the peoples of the earth. It's my turn to engage the nations.
20. I affirm that the strategy of Jesus for world conquest is spiritual multiplication. It's my turn to produce and multiply more Kingdom laborers.

Signature _____

Date _____

BATON PASSING AS A KINGDOM LABORER

A group of police recruits were in class ready to take their final examination. They were asked by their instructor how they would respond to the following city-wide disaster:

A young boy is drowning in a nearby lake. A woman's purse has been stolen on a main street downtown. A car has just struck a fire hydrant and water is spraying out of control. And, an attempted bank robbery has turned into a hostage crisis.

One by one the recruits were called upon to stand to their feet and verbalize a plan of action. Finally, at the back of the room, one recruit dared to be honest, saying, "Remove uniform; mingle with crowd."

As we look around us or watch the latest newsfeed, we are tempted to respond similarly. The path of least resistance in the face of desperate need is to remove our name badge (or the cross from around our neck) and blend with the crowd. If Jesus were walking the earth today, looking at the masses of our generation, He'd likely draw the same conclusion that He did 2,000 years ago in Matthew 9:37-38: "The harvest is plentiful, but the laborers are few. Ask the Lord of the harvest, therefore, to send out laborers into his harvest field."

When Jesus gazed at the masses (a microcosm of the world's population), He drew—not six or eight complex steps toward a solution—

but one, simple conclusion about what those in his sightline needed: laborers. What an intriguing word. What a compelling term to encompass all that was necessary to meet the needs of people.

He told His disciples—whom He had already converted from laypeople to laborers—to pray that God would "send" more laborers into the vast harvest fields of human need. The word "send" was a passionate Aramaic word. It is the same word used in scripture to describe how Jesus "cast out" wicked spirits from a demonized person. It literally means "to thrust" or "to boot out." Jesus was commanding us to pray that God would "boot out" laborers into His ripened and ready harvest field!

How crucial was the need for more laborers to Jesus? While Jesus prayed often, He rarely issued prayer requests during His ministry. This was one of the few: Pray that the Lord of the harvest would send out laborers! He apparently took this seriously. What do you think?

In fact, the primary purpose in Jesus' selection of His twelve disciples centered around this very issue. His objective wasn't to help them feel closer to God, or experience "goosebumps" from watching Him heal the blind. It was to turn them into Kingdom laborers. Do you remember what He said when He recruited them? "Follow me, and I will send you out to fish for people" (Matthew 4:19). The call came with the commitment to follow Jesus and to labor in God's harvest fields.

So, just what is a "laborer?" If you check the dictionary, you'll find this definition.

lā-bər : toil or tribute offered for a cause; it can make weary, but also produces fruit.

What a concise yet candid summary. In this case, the cause is the advancement of God's rule and reign on earth. "Thy kingdom come" was the objective of Jesus' labor.

This labor can take on many forms. It may be done in your church. It may be behind-the-scenes service offered in a soup kitchen downtown. It may be investing in one person over an extended period of time. It could be teaching a Bible study, sharing Christ with your neighbors, demonstrating Christ's love on a basketball court, or washing the frail, wrinkled body of an elderly person in a retirement home. And, it might just be moving to a cross-cultural setting and ministering to an unreached people group.

Regardless of your assignment, some common characteristics mark every effective laborer.

We are convinced that all fruitful laborers:

1. Love Jesus Christ intimately and are discipled by Him.
2. Use their gifts and resources to advance God's kingdom.
3. Reproduce more laborers for Kingdom multiplication.

None of these characteristics require that you be in full-time, vocational ministry. Some laborers, of course, will be; but it is crucial for most to stay in the marketplace of their life and work to serve as a fully devoted laborer for Christ. Everyday life in everyday places is where the majority of people who need Jesus are located. What better place is there to be!

It is remarkable to consider that if we all would commit to becoming laborers right where we live, the Great Commission could be fulfilled. Remember, this was Jesus' solution to the needy state of the multitudes: laborers.

Stop and evaluate your life in light of this definition of a laborer. How are you doing? Are you using your gifts in a strategic way? Can you point to how God's kingdom is advancing through your laborership? Are you reproducing more Kingdom laborers?

No matter where you are in your spiritual journey, you can become a fruitful Kingdom laborer. It may require some confession and a step of commitment to move you from sedentary spiritual sitting to harvest field serving. That's totally okay. Jesus is kind and patient. He's been ready and waiting for you to begin. Isn't it time to get started in becoming a part of the answer to Jesus' "more laborers" prayer?

A RUNNER'S GUIDE TO RACING

We pray you've been challenged, inspired, and equipped through the stories in this book and have wholeheartedly embraced "The Laborer's Declaration." But living out the "It's my turn" affirmation statements in that declaration won't always be easy. Every commitment must be followed by a process of growth to bear fruit over the long haul. As Dawson Trotman said, "Remember, making a decision is 5 percent; 95 percent is following through. God is not glorified…unless the decision is confirmed by a Christian life that follows it."

Here are a few practical suggestions to encourage you as you follow through on your commitment and take your place in the relay race of human history.

1. Expect opposition from the enemy.

Your decision to be a committed Kingdom laborer has not gone unnoticed by Satan. And when soldiers get closer to the front lines of battle, the fighting gets more intense. It's no different in spiritual battle. "Your enemy the devil prowls around like a roaring lion," 1 Peter 5:8 tells us, "looking for someone to devour."

You have nothing to fear, because "the One who is in you is greater than the one who is in the world" (1 John 4:4). At the same time, it would be naive and foolish to ignore the reality of spiritual warfare. Satan would love to render you ineffective in the battle for human souls. Remember to put on the full armor of God daily (Ephesians 6:10-18). Trust in the love and grace of God and His Spirit at work within you. Know that, "He who has begun a good work in you," (Philippians 1:6) "will be faithful to complete it!"

2. Beware of the "Elijah Syndrome."

After the great victory on Mount Carmel over the prophets of Baal in 1 Kings 18, Elijah hit bottom. Jezebel threatened him, he panicked and ran for his life. Alone at Mount Horeb, Elijah pleaded his case to God: "I have been very zealous for the LORD God Almighty," he said. "The Israelites have rejected your covenant, broken down your altars, and put our prophets to death with the sword. I am the only one left, and now they are trying to kill me, too" (1 Kings 19:10).

Elijah was convinced that he was the only one faithful to God. The pressure of opposition got to Elijah and he bought the lie Satan continues to sell today. You, too, may be tempted to look around and believe you are the only remaining faithful believer. But listen to God's perspective on Elijah's situation: "I reserve seven thousand in Israel—whose knees have not bowed down to Baal and whose mouths have not kissed him" (1 Kings 19:18).

Despite appearances, you are not alone. God has placed His Holy Spirit within you, and, He continues to raise up and assemble laborers in every corner of the world to walk with you. Ask God to guide you to other Kingdom laborers in your area or on-line. Encourage one another as you work together to build God's Kingdom.

3. Deal with rejection graciously.

Some people will not understand the commitments you have made in "The Laborer's Declaration." Laborers from every generation have been branded as radicals and fanatics. Even members of your family, friends, church, or campus group may find it difficult to accept your newfound passion in pursuing God's purpose for your life.

The apostle Paul gives laborers of every generation some important words of instruction on this subject. In his second letter to the Corinthians, Paul listed many of the hardships he faced in the process of obedience. His list included dishonor, bad reports, and being regarded as an impostor. Added to those adversities, Paul was imprisoned, endured beatings, and suffered many sleepless nights! In this same passage, however, Paul emphasized the importance of "purity, understanding, patience...kindness and sincere love" (2 Corinthians 6:6). As you face rejection and misunderstanding, ask God to empower you with the fruit of the Holy Spirit. And with all you say and do, "put on love," as Paul instructs in Colossians 3:14. Eventually, skeptics and critics may be won over by the grace and love they see portrayed in your life. Regardless, your love, commitment, and willingness to face struggle and hardship will please God. And God is, and will always be, enough.

4. Balance your zeal with wisdom.

Clearly, passion is necessary in carrying out your commitment to be a laborer. Paul urged the church in Rome to be passionate, saying, "Never be lacking in zeal, but keep your spiritual fervor, serving the Lord" (Romans 12:11). God's Kingdom today is in desperate need of passionate laborers who aren't lacking in zeal. Equally, zeal without spiritual maturity can be harmful. The wisdom-writer warns, "it is not good to have zeal without knowledge, nor to be hasty and miss the way" (Proverbs 19:2).

Seek out godly counsel and other mature believers. Strive to grow and develop your ministry skills. Cooperate with existing ministry structures whenever possible. Season your words with love. And beware of alienating those around you by plowing ahead without first gaining wisdom. Become a good listener and learner as you also engage as a passionate doer.

A Runner's Guide to Racing

5. Guard your heart against pride.

Becoming a sincere and committed Kingdom laborer will bring favor, blessing, and opportunity to your life. Expect God to use you to advance His Kingdom! As you begin to experience results, however, you may be tempted to take credit or seek recognition for what God has accomplished through you. Be on guard not to rob God of glory rightly belonging to Him. Pride is a killer. It can sideline you and move you off course as quickly as anything. Remember Peter's words: "God opposes the proud but gives grace to the humble. Humble yourselves, therefore, under God's mighty hand, that He may lift you up in due time" (1 Peter 5:5-6). Humility is key. Humble Kingdom laborers, guided and empowered by "God's mighty hand," advance His Kingdom most efficiently and effectively.

6. Stay the course as your emotions rise and fall.

One of the most common statements your skeptics will make is that your newfound vision and passion will never last. "It's just a fad," some might say. "Youthful zeal—wait and see." While it's true that your feelings will come and go, being a Kingdom laborer is not about riding an emotional wave into heaven. Life is a good teacher, and reality checks will come. So will spiritual lows and discouragements. Don't give up! Love and faith are more than just feelings.

Stay the course. Keep your eyes focused on Jesus through all the successes and failures. Like thousands of others who have gone before you, you can persevere in your commitment to live a life of total surrender to the cause of Christ. God will give you the grace and strength needed to stand against any forces seeking to undo you.

7. Don't let failure discourage you from running the race.

At one time or another, you will most likely ask yourself in a time of discouragement, "What's the use?" Stress, temptation, and fatigue you will push you toward making mistakes, suffering setbacks, and even failing—perhaps miserably. But don't give up! Let God nurture you, receive His grace, and get your feet moving again. Remember that when you are weak, His strength is made perfect (2 Corinthians 12:9). Draw upon the power of the Holy Spirit and share your journey with trusted co-laborers and mentors. Consider how you can "spur one another on toward love and good deeds...all the more as you see the Day approaching" (Hebrews 10:24-25).

The road of Kingdom laborership is often bumpy. Running on freshly paved roads and smooth trails is great but rarely the norm. Expect potholes, speed bumps, hurdles, and detours on your laboring marathon. You will learn to depend on God and trust His navigation as the faithful laborers written about in this book did.

Stay in the race—it's so worth it! As you keep your eyes firmly fixed on Jesus and run the race set before you with perseverance, you will finish strong. What's more, you will one day take your place among the faithful "cloud of witnesses" who devoted their lives to the cause of Christ.

You've remembered these laborers. You've considered the outcome of their way of life. Now imitate their faith. Why? Because...

It's your turn!

GETTING THE MOST OUT OF THIS BOOK

Loving God, Loving People

Loving God and loving people have always been at the heart of Kingdom laboring. The two are inseparable. We cannot love God without loving people. God's love can't simply be enjoyed or possessed and never shared. His love is so rich and deep that to experience it compels us to share it and express it outwardly in ways that can be heard, seen, felt, and experienced. Equally, loving people requires an ongoing love of God. It's not that we can't do good things for people without loving God, it's just that whatever we do will never be adequate or complete. Our care and solutions will never satisfy their greatest need or help them reach their fullest potential.

To love God is to love people. To love people is to love them in a more complete way out of God's love alive within us. That's why we continue to beat the drum that Kingdom laboring is about a heart on fire AND a life on purpose. A heart up-close to God sets a heart ablaze. The closer we get to God, the warmer, brighter, and more beautiful we become. Our lives begin to reflect God's love and character. We begin to see what God sees and do what God does. God's love begins to clarify and shape a life on purpose. We begin to focus our

Getting the Most Out of This Book

lives on what matters most to God. And what matters most to God is people! A life on purpose is to love people out of a deep, ongoing, and abiding heart on fire love for God.

Every baton-passing runner in this book has a heart on fire, life on purpose story. None of them are simply hearts on fire people or life on purpose people. Each of them loved God intimately and served Him passionately. As we've already stated: loving God and loving people are inseparable.

While we've assigned ten of the biographies as hearts on fire and ten as lives on purpose, we've done so only to highlight and illustrate aspects of the entire hearts on fire, lives on purpose life we are all called to live. To love God well is to love people well. To love people well can only be done by loving God well. Each of these runners passed a baton of faith out of both their love for God and their love of people. As you read and engage God through this book and study, may you also love people well, because you continue to love God well.

Read, Engage, Commit, Get Active

This book is a tool. Tools are made to be used to make things better, stronger, more effective, complete. We hope you see this book as a tool to make you a better laborer and baton-passer for God's Kingdom. Here's a suggested way to engage It's My Turn:

Read

For each chapter, begin by reading the biographical story. Let the story make its way into your heart, mind, and imagination. Put yourself in the setting of the story as much as possible. What might you be wearing? What are the smells in the air and the taste of the food? Where would you be in the crowd, or on the boat, or near the battle?

Consider also, how you might feel or what you might think if you are the hero or heroine in the story. Ponder what you might be thinking or feeling if you're another less noble figure in the narrative.

Give your experience even greater nuance by asking, "Where is Jesus while these things are happening?"

Realize also that the hero or heroine highlighted has much longer and intricate story (just as the one reading it does). While we pull out a piece of their story here and there to illustrate or examine, God has been orchestrating, growing, and shaping them over a lifetime. They didn't arrive where they are overnight. Neither should that be our expectation.

Engage

After reading the biography, engage the questions at the end of the chapter. They are designed to engage the story, engage God's Word, and engage your life. To engage is to get involved in, to participate. It means get active in the process. Don't be just a reader of a book but be a doer of God's Word. Your goal is not to complete an assignment but to meet the Living Lord. God has the same power to love you and employ you in His Kingdom work as much as the person you're reading about and studying. Believe it!

There's a section at the end of the chapter called For Further Reflection and Engagement. It's an added opportunity to engage God and the book. For those who journal, it a great place to utilize the questions provided.

Commit

Action requires commitment. It takes a deliberate act of the heart and will to move from answers on a paper to action in life. Make a commitment to God to follow through with what you say you'll do. Even greater, make a commitment that you'll follow through with what you hear God asking you to say and do. When God asks or says, it's a matter of obedience. Remember, to love God is to obey Him (John 14:15).

At the end of the book is The Laborer's Declaration. It's an opportunity to make and mark your commitment to God in becoming a

Getting the Most Out of This Book

baton-passer for your generation. The vow you will be making is a most solemn one. Make your decision carefully and prayerfully. Consider including others in your time of commitment. You may want to include a time of praise and worship, commissioning prayer, food and celebration.

Get Active

Love is a verb, an action word. Get active loving God and loving people. Your goal isn't busyness or religious activity, however. People aren't commodities to be won, collected, or manipulated. Your goal is for others to know and be known by the One who created them, loves them, wants to reconcile and free them. Jesus was a great inviter. He welcomed and invited people to a life God always intended for them. It's our privilege to do likewise. That's a joyous outcome worth our time, resources, energy, and action.

GROUP STUDY TIPS

If you are planning to study this book in a large or small group setting, here's one way to structure your time together. The following outline will allow flexibility in facilitating a one- to two-hour gathering.

Mingle (15-30 minutes)

If time allows, build in some space for mingling. 15 to 30 minutes before group discussion will give time for people to catch up on their week and for relationships to naturally deepen. Consider having members of your group volunteer to bring snacks, share a meal, or bring dessert. More responsibility brings greater ownership.

Consider asking a question or two that might break the ice and encourage the group to share freely. For example, "How about we quickly go around the room and say a color that best describes your day?" The questions are limitless. Any question that will get the group talking will be great.

Engage (30-45 minutes)

Begin with prayer and ask God to be the real facilitator of your

Group Study Tips

time together. Ask Holy Spirit to open your hearts and minds to all that He has for you as you meet.

Using one, some, or all the questions from the current week's Engage sections at the end of the chapter, allow discussion to unfold in natural, unforced ways. Read the listed Scriptures out loud in your group as you discuss the related questions. The questions are there to serve you, not the other way around. Let Holy Spirit set the agenda as you go. Your goal is not to answer a set number of questions but to allow God to have His way in each of you as you go. Do your best to make sure everyone feels welcome, is seen, and has opportunity to speak.

Challenge (15 minutes)

Take some time to talk about any action steps people committed to as a result of the study. Talk about any potential fears or obstacles individuals are facing. If needed, pause and pray for someone facing discouragement or needing strength, courage, forgiveness, etc.

Challenge and encourage those committing to taking a next step in sharing the gospel or trusting God in something new.

Wrap-up (5-30 minutes)

Gauge your closing time. Ending your gathering in prayer is great! If time allows, consider these additional possibilities:

- Share prayer requests.
- Invite the group to share what God has been teaching them (in the study or elsewhere).
- Have someone share a 5- to 10-minute snapshot of his or her God-story. Encourage and pray for them after they do.

End the gathering with a one-minute overview of your next gathering.

ADDITIONAL QUESTIONS & CHALLENGES TO ENGAGE

Keith Green

Engage the Story
On several occasions in Keith's life, he risked vulnerability, popularity, and income by challenging others to greater intimacy with Jesus. Have you risked anything in your life so that others might know Jesus in a deeper way? If so, how?

Engage God's Word
In John 4:24, Jesus said true worship occurs in "spirit and in truth." What does Jesus mean by that statement? How can you practice this in your life?

Carefully read Psalm 139:23-24. Ask God to expose anything in you that is keeping you from greater intimacy with Him. Ask God to help you overcome any barriers He reveals.

Additional Questions & Challenges to Engage

Josiah Henson

Engage the Story
Josiah left his family and risked his freedom in order to rescue others from slavery. What motivated him to make such a sacrifice? What might you do with family and freedom on the line?

At times, Josiah felt forsaken by God. Like King David of Israel, he wondered where God was in his trouble and discouragement. Have you ever felt that way? Who or what brought you to a better place?

Engage God's Word
Read Exodus 3:1-14. What is Moses' reaction to God's call? What does he fear? What is God's assurance? How do you relate to Moses in this story? Discuss what is truly necessary to make a Kingdom impact in our world (see Acts 4:13).

Engage My Life
Kingdom laborers are disciples of Jesus who enact His very heart in our world. While God has called all laborers to fight for spiritual freedom, He is calling some to also fight for the physical freedom of the enslaved! If God is leading you to do more, research ways that people are being enslaved worldwide, and how you can get involved.

Florence Nightingale

Engage the Story
Arriving at the makeshift hospital in the Crimean Peninsula, Florence found deplorable conditions and discouraging organization. Though disheartening, she pressed on. What might discourage you from

Additional Questions & Challenges to Engage

continuing what God has called you to? What will enable you to persevere when obstacles come?

Engage God's Word
On one difficult occasion, after some soldiers had died just after receiving treatment, Florence said, "I am weary of this hopeless work." Yet, she still continued in her task. How might Galatians 6:2 and 9 spur us on to continue the race when faced with times of weariness and discouragement?

Engage My Life
Florence saw her work for the Lord all the way to completion. She stayed behind after the war to care for wounded soldiers until they could return home. Do you have something God has given you that needs completed? Commit today to finishing whatever God has started in and through you.

C.T. Studd

Engage the Story
In what ways have you seen God "laugh at impossibilities," either in your own life or in the lives of others? Why do you think God likes to use unlikely people to accomplish His purposes?

Engage God's Word
Read 1 John 5:2-4 and John 14:15. How are obedience and love connected? Why do you think God places such a high value on obedience?

Read 1 John 5:3. John says that to love God is to what? And that his commands are not what? Consider why so many bristle or hesitate

Additional Questions & Challenges to Engage

when asked to obey God. Does obedience seem burdensome to you? Why or why not?

Engage My Life
Take time to quiet your heart and mind before God. Ask God to give you a Kingdom assignment (large or small). Whatever you hear God asking, do it. Rest assured, God will never ask you to do something that violates His Word, His character, or love.

C.T. believed strongly in spiritual baton-passing, mentoring others in the faith for spiritual multiplication. Who is God asking you to mentor? If, for you, that's a new concept, seek out someone spiritually mature and ask them to help you grow in your understanding and practice of spiritual multiplication. You can visit ForgeForward.org/Resources for helpful spiritual multiplication tools.

Luis Palau

Engage the Story
Luis was only ten-years old when his father died. His family, once affluent, became poor. Both he and his wife, Pat, battled cancer. How do you think these events shaped Luis' life and ministry? How might they have shaped yours?

Luis once said, "Only God can change people." What do you think he meant? How does that statement influence the way you see evangelism?

Luis became restless as a missionary. While he was faithful and ministry was fruitful, he knew God had made him for a different Kingdom purpose. Have you ever been restless in life and ministry? Would you be willing to leave a job or profession where you feel you are effective if you sensed God leading you to something different? What factors would lead you to your final decision?

Engage God's Word
Read Romans 8:37-39. This was a favorite passage of Luis's mother. Considering the many hard circumstances Luis and his family faced, how might it have been difficult to believe this truth? Equally, how comforting must it be for him to know that through it all, it really is true and dependable?

Read Romans 12:1-3. How do you see Luis's life in light of these verses? How do these verses impact your life and laboring?

Engage My Life
"Evangelism is not an option for the Christian life." What does sharing the good news of life in Christ look like for you? Does it fit or feel uncomfortable? Does it come easily or with fear and obstacles? Talk to Jesus about what it looks like to share His good news in ways that look just like you.

What we value most often informs our actions. As you look at your life, is sharing the gospel message with others currently a high value for you? Is sharing the gospel something that you have done in the last month or two? If not, what steps can you take to increase this value in your life? Take note that the unique gifts and talents that God has given you often work together to make you a very effective kingdom laborer.

George Mueller

Engage the Story
George could have gone to Baghdad as a missionary instead of

Additional Questions & Challenges to Engage

serving in Bristol. He realized, however, the need in Bristol was significant. "God has given me a mission field right here, and I will live and die in it," he said. What constitutes a mission field? What unconventional "mission fields" might be just around the corner from you?

As you consider all of the possible mission fields in your life, what do you notice? From a biblical perspective is there anywhere where you are not on mission? How can you live a life of purpose recognizing that everywhere you are is a mission field?

If your support network disapproved of what God had called you to, how would you respond to them? Would you, like George, find another way to proceed with your plans? Would you be tempted to reroute God's calling to please your family, friends, or funding sources?

George constantly prayed for God to do the impossible. How do you think someone gets to that depth of faith? Do you find yourself praying for big or seemingly impossible things, why or why not?

Engage God's Word
Meditate on James 1:27 (mull it over, let it saturate your heart and thoughts, savor it). What do you hear God saying to you about orphans and widows? What is your response?

Read Hebrews 11. Why is it impossible to please God without faith? What do the people listed in the "Hall of Faith" teach you about "having confidence in what we hope for and assurance about what we do not see"?

Engage My Life
George didn't just wake up one day with some miracle gift of faith. God grew and increased George's faith as George trusted God, one act of faith at a time. What do you think is needed to increase your faith

in what God can do? Ask God to teach you how faithful, powerful, and trustworthy He is.

George continually depended on God through prayer. What are some areas of your life that you need to prayerfully depend on God and quit depending on yourself?

Research local, national, and international ministries that provide for orphans, immigrants, and the homeless. Prayerfully discover ways to get actively involved through your prayers, presence, and financial gifts.

Watchman Nee

Engage the Story
Persecution may be physical but also includes discrimination, ridicule, and insults for the sake of Christ and His mission. Have you experienced any of these where you live and serve?

Engage God's Word
Read James 1:2-12. Make a list of the advice James gives for those who are "scattered among the nations." Make your list as if James is sitting with you before you leave for your mission assignment.

Read Jeremiah 31:3-9. Watchman lived his name. He became "the watchman who would sound the warning and deliver the gospel to the people of China." As you engage God through the Jeremiah passage, what do you hear Him saying to you about your name and Kingdom assignment?
Engage My Life

Many see suffering as something to avoid at all costs. Watchman saw suffering as a way to depend on Christ. How have you viewed and dealt with any physical, emotional, mental, spiritual, or relational suffering? How have you trusted and depended on God in those trials? If not God, where do you turn when you face those trials? As you face trials in the future How might you learn to grow deeper in your trust and dependence on God and avoid going to other sources for comfort?

Amy Carmichael

Engage the Story
As a youngster, Amy rejected the dark brown eyes God had given her and longed instead for blue eyes. With her brown eyes, however, she was later able to go inside the Hindu temples to rescue children. Is there any unchangeable feature of your own body or personality that you don't care for? How do you see God potentially using the specific way He designed you for his Kingdom purpose?

After Amy's book sales had passed the half million mark in fifteen languages and Braille, she learned that a magazine article had described her books as "popular." She responded, "Popular? Lord, is that what these books written out of the heat of the battle are? Popular? O Lord, burn the paper to ashes if that be true." How might you have responded to large book sales and popularity?

Engage God's Word
In 1886, Amy was gripped by Jude 1:24-25. Why do you think it moved her? Read it slowly 2-3 times. How does it stir, move, or compel you?

Engage My Life
What's a simple pleasure you can give up for a period of time in order to practice denying yourself for the sake of Christ? Could be as small

as a daily cup of coffee to something much more costly in time, enjoyment, or resources. Replace that activity or item by spending time with the Lord, seeking His plans and purposes. Whatever money you might have saved, consider donating it to a ministry that works with overlooked and undervalued children.

Humility is not thinking less of yourself; rather, it's thinking about yourself less and others more. Amy demonstrated such humility. How is humility reflected in your daily life? What's one practical thing you can do in your life to practice thinking more highly of others than yourself?

John Hyde

Engage the Story
It was what John deemed "failure" (lack of spiritual conversions) that led him to a life of fervent prayer. How have you seen failure, actual or perceived, inspire prayer? In what ways might God use failure to help you grow?

Have you ever felt a burden to pray for someone or something? Why do you think God lays such burdens on specific people?

Engage God's Word
Read Colossians 4:2-4. What does it mean to be "watchful and thankful" in prayer?

At age twenty-seven John faced an unexpected giant that threatened to destroy the effectiveness of his prayer life: pride of spiritual achievement. What does 1 Corinthians 4:7 say about the things you are tempted to call your accomplishments?

Additional Questions & Challenges to Engage

Engage My Life
At age seventeen, John discovered that the purpose of prayer is not to get from God what we want, but to allow God to receive from us what He wants. What does He want from you? How does God want to align your heart with what He's up to? Ask Him. Listen.

William Wilberforce

Engage the Story
When people are critical of your convictions, what kind of impact does that have on you? Do you turn to God for strength to help you persevere, or do you succumb to the pressures of shame and pleasing others? Why do think that is?

Engage God's Word
Read Micah 6:8. What does God mean that He requires us to "act justly, love mercy, and walk humbly" with Him?

Sit with Psalm 137. The context is the Israelites enslaved by the Babylonians. Read it thoughtfully and carefully from the point of view of the one held captive. What is God teaching you as you read and listen? How does that impact the way you think about, pray for, and engage those around the globe who are mistreated unjustly?

Engage My Life
Lord, I am most discouraged, fearful, and undone in the task you set before me when… (fill in the blank)

Additional Questions & Challenges to Engage

Susanna Wesley

Engage the Story
The day to day duties of raising ten children would have filled Susanna's days with numerous responsibilities. Yet, she placed a high priority on her relationship with God. What evidence do you see that up-close time with God was vital to her?

Engage God's Word
Read I Corinthians 12:12-27. How does this passage give perspective to Susanna's life? How does it give perspective to your life?

Engage My Life
Susanna was content with how God made her and the purposes He had for her. God was enough. Honestly assess your life and attitudes. Do you look for ways God can use you in your everyday uniqueness, or are you always looking for something more elevated, flashy, or unique?

Consider coming along someone like Susanna who selflessly serves others behind the scenes. Think about a way you can ease their load, give them a respite, and encourage them. Let them know God sees them and what they do is highly important to God's Kingdom.

Eric Liddell

Engage the Story
Eric shared his story in all kinds of unique venues. What are some creative places and ways to share about Jesus in non-traditional ways where you live?

Additional Questions & Challenges to Engage

When Eric refused to run on Sunday, he was accused of being unpatriotic and legalistic. Was he? What are some actions done or left undone in relation to following Jesus that could be considered unpatriotic or legalistic today?

Engage God's Word
Read Colossians 3:17, 1 Peter 2:9, Acts 4:13, and Acts 8:1, 4. Do these passages communicate that full-time vocational ministry positions (Pastors, Evangelists, Missionaries, etc.) are God's highest calling or are they communicating another truth?

In 1 Corinthians 9:19-27 Paul the Apostle reveals some degree of flexibility is required to "be all things to all people" for the sake of the mission. We also know that Paul was a man of strong conviction. We have also discovered how convictional and immovable Eric was regarding Sundays. When it comes to advancing God's Kingdom, in what ways should your life be flexible, and in what ways immovable?

Engage My Life
Eric wrote, "The bravest moment of a person's life is the moment when he looks at himself objectively without wincing, without complaining. However, self-examination that does not result in action is dangerous. What am I going to do about what I see? The action called for is surrender—of ourselves to God." During objective self-examination, what might you be inclined to wince, squirm, or complain about? How can you practically surrender these to Jesus and begin looking upward to Him more than you look inward?

Martin Luther

Engage the Story
Have you ever felt so strongly about something that you were

compelled to go way out of your comfort zone to make it happen or do something about it? Have you ever felt the conviction to do something but then backed out? What happened?

What are some important issues in our world today that require Christians to stand for truth even if their views are unpopular or opposed?

Engage God's Word
Read Romans 1:17 and explain it in your own words.

Martin faced criticism for his teaching of solo fides (faith alone), sola gratin (grace alone), and solos Christus (Christ alone). What truth does Ephesians 2:8-9 teach?

Engage My Life
Martin believed so deeply in living by the truth of God's Word that he was willing to face the threats of imprisonment and death. How willing are you to live by and for the truth of God's Word?

Dwight Moody

Engage the Story
Dwight once said, "Before my conversion I worked toward the cross, but since then I have worked from the cross; then I worked to be saved, now I work because I am saved." What do you think he meant by this? Try to concretely define the difference.

Do you have a hard time sharing your faith with others? If so, what are some of the obstacles that hold you back? How can you work to overcome these?

Additional Questions & Challenges to Engage

Engage God's Word
Read Matthew 10. What do your findings teach you about sharing the message of Jesus?

Read Matthew 28:19-20. This passage is commonly referred to as the "Great Commission." Though it seems like just one command, it includes two things that we are called to do and one thing that God promises to do. Identify these different parts. What about this passage encourages you or excites you? What about this passage makes you afraid or uneasy?

Engage My Life
Henry Varley, a preacher friend, casually remarked, "The world has yet to see what God will do with a man fully consecrated to Him." After pondering those words for weeks, Dwight resolved that by the Holy Spirit's power, he would be that man. Later, as he watched 200 young men respond to the gospel, Moody said, "My God, this is enough to live for." Can you put into a single sentence what you are living for? What would an objective observer say you are living for?

Dwight and a friend started a Sunday School in an abandoned boxcar. If creativity is seeing what others have over-looked, ask God to give you one creative observation that would help in reaching someone with the gospel.

Hudson Taylor

Engage the Story
Hudson was intrigued with maps and adventures from a very young age. God planted seeds just waiting to be watered and grow. What things have captured your heart, mind, and imagination since you

were young? Do you think God might have been planting some seeds in you for serving His Kingdom now?

Three years past from the time Hudson clearly heard God's call for him to go to China and actually boarding a ship to go. Resources and training opportunities were scarce, but Hudson was determined. How did he choose to spend his time during those three years? Likewise, are you stewarding your time? How so?

Engage God's Word
Recalling the minister's comment, "Ah, my boy, as you grow older you will get wiser than that. Such an idea would do very well in the days when Christ himself was on earth, but not now," read Acts 1:8, Matthew 6:33, and Hebrews 13:8. How do these passages inform Hudson's critic?

The Book of Acts is sometimes referred to as The Acts of Prayer. Using a word search tool, see how many times a form of "pray" is used in the Book of Acts. When you're finished, think about what this means for the importance of prayer in spreading the gospel.

Engage My Life
Upon dissecting a contaminated body with other lab students, Hudson accidentally pricked his finger. The supervisor told him to go home as fast as he could and put his affairs in order, saying, "You are a dead man." But God healed him through a slow recovery. Has God spared you because of Kingdom plans He has for you? Give Him thanks. If you aren't sure, praise and thank God still. He has certainly sent "angels unaware" to spare you throughout your lifetime.

Additional Questions & Challenges to Engage

Jarena Lee

Engage the Story
While Jarena heard a clear call to preach she waited eight years out of respect for her church. Would you have waited so long? Why or why not? Do you believe she did the right thing? Why?

Engage God's Word
Read Esther 4:16 and 7:1-10. Esther was a biblical heroine who saved the Jewish people. She is recognized for her strength, bravery, and dignity. Compare Jarena and Esther's stories. How did God use these women of faith to advance His Kingdom?

Engage My Life
Jarena struggled early in life with feeling worthless, unwanted, and unfit to be alive. God intervened and spared her life for incredible Kingdom service. Do you know anyone feeling overlooked and undervalued who is struggling? Pray for them. Encourage them. Be present in his or her life. God is in no way done with them.

Read 2 Corinthians 11:23-33. Both Jarena and Paul the Apostle faced extreme barriers and opposition to their God-given callings to proclaim the Gospel. How willing are you to lovingly navigate difficult barriers and opposition to obey God's calling for your life?

John Paton

Engage the Story
When the Sacred Men tried to show the strength of their god by attempting to take John's life, John trusted God would reveal that God alone is in control of life and power. How have you seen God's

character and power put on display in your life or in the lives of others?

John dealt with spiritual darkness and spiritual warfare constantly. Some Christian traditions talk about these realities, others do not. What is your understanding of spiritual darkness and warfare? What is your biblical knowledge of these things?

Engage God's Word
Read Matthew 6:5-15. Jesus gave us a model for prayer. How does this prayer shape the life of a missionary? How does it shape your daily life?

John was engaged in "spiritual warfare." Read 2 Corinthians 4:4, Revelation 12:11, and Ephesians 6:10-20. What principles do these passages provide in confronting Satan, our enemy?

Engage My Life
In his later years, John influenced young people to serve in missions. Do you know anyone God might have His hand on regarding missionary service? Consider having a conversation with them. Ask, "Have you ever felt called or compelled to serve God's Kingdom as a missionary?" If they answer "yes," intentionally slow down, listen, pray, encourage, and seek out how you can support their next steps.

William Booth

Engage the Story
When warned that he was physically at risk in working with the poor, William replied, "Unfit? Of course, I am unfit in myself. But in the strength God gives me, I am going to do the thing God has called me to do." Have you disqualified yourself from serving the Lord, because

Additional Questions & Challenges to Engage

others talked you out of it or discouraged you? What might others see as limitations in your life but not so by God?

Hundreds of young people, as officers in the "army" William founded, promised, "For Christ's sake, to feed the poor, clothe the naked, love the unlovable, and befriend the friendless." What do you think compelled them to take such a vow?

Engage God's Word
How does the famous "love chapter" challenge our daily caring for the poor and disadvantaged? Read I Corinthians 13:1-8, paying particular attention to verse 3. What does it mean to "love"?

Engage My Life
In William's story, a writer compares two people. Re-read. Pause. Reflect. Ask God which of the two your life most resembles. Be honest with God and yourself in the assessment. Spend time talking with God about having your life reflect His heart in caring for the overlooked, undervalued, oppressed, and disadvantaged in the world.

William brought the gospel message to the streets with innovative open-air meetings. How are you creatively sharing the gospel in your everyday places of influence? Wherever you step foot, keep your eyes open for ways you can creatively proclaim Jesus.

William Carey

Engage the Story
William was a pioneering missionary in his respect for preserving a nation's culture. When the first person was converted in India, William said that the new believer "became a Christian, not a European." What do you think he meant by this? Why should we

Additional Questions & Challenges to Engage

emphasize people changing their beliefs rather than their cultures? What are the characteristics that should be true of all Christians, regardless of culture?

As a young man, William worked as a shoemaker. He made a map of the world on the wall over his cobbler's bench so he could pray as he worked. He prayed for God's movement across the globe. What do you think of his idea? Are there unique ways you could pray for God's movement among the nations? Consider choosing several nations by the end of the day and pray for the gospel to advance there.

Engage God's Word
Revelation 7:9 describes "a great multitude... from every nation, tribe, people and language, standing before the throne." Why do you think the Bible places such an emphasis on the diversity of people in heaven? What can you learn about God's character from seeing His desire for all nations to know and be saved?

William thanked God for the daily regularity with which his parents drilled him on scripture. "My mind was furnished with themes, which afterwards were often influential on my heart, when I had little leisure." Read a few sections of Psalm 119, noting how often God's law, statutes, precepts, and commands are mentioned. What do you discover about the value of Scripture?

Engage My Life
Late in life, William said to an admirer, "You have been speaking about Dr. Carey. When I am gone, say nothing about Dr. Carey—speak about Dr. Carey's Savior!" Write down what you'd like said about your Savior when you're gone.

Additional Questions & Challenges to Engage

Dawson Trotman

Engage the Story
Dawson believed that a discipling relationship culminates in the new believer bringing someone else to faith in Christ. According to that standard, have you been discipled? Have you discipled anyone?

Trotman drowned while rescuing a young girl who had fallen from a boat. In an obituary, Time magazine described him as "always holding someone up." Based on your life, what might be said about you in your obituary?

Engage God's Word
Read Mark 1:17-18 and Mark 1:13-19. Does the church today value the hard work of one-one-one disciple-making and mentoring in the same way that Jesus did? Why or why not?

How does Jesus disciple? Consider reading through one of the four Gospels and noting how Jesus taught, modeled, and motivated His disciples to follow Him and serve the Kingdom.

Engage My Life
Dawson heavily emphasized scripture memory because of the positive impact it had on his own life and faith. What does Psalm 119:11 teach us to do? Select a verse you have never memorized. Write it down and memorize it now. Learn it and "hide it in your heart." Ask God to bring that Scripture to your mind when it's needed. Create a plan to regularly memorize new Scripture.

BIBLIOGRAPHY

LISTED AS RECOMMENDED READING IN BIOGRAPHIES

Bailey, Faith Coxe. D.L. Moody, The Greatest Evangelist of the Nineteenth Century. Chicago: The Moody Bible Institute. 1987.

Bailey, Faith Coxe. George Mueller: He Dared to Trust God for the Needs of Countless Orphans. Chicago: The Moody Bible Institute, 1958.

Bainton, Roland. Here I Stand: A Life of Martin Luther. Nashville: Abingdon, 1978.

Begbie, Harold. William Booth, Founder of the Salvation Army. New York: McMillan Company, 1920.

Brock, Jared A. The Road to Dawn: Josiah Henson and the Story That Sparked the Civil War. New York: Public Affairs, 2018.

Byrum, Bessie G. John G. Paton, Hero of the South Seas. Gospel Trumpet Company, 1924.

Dallimore, Arnold. Susanna Wesley: The Mother of John & Charles Wesley. Grand Rapids: Baker Books, 1993.

DeRusha, Michelle. 50 Women Every Christian Should Know: Learning from Heroines of the Faith. Grand Rapids: Baker Books, 2014.

Dorsett, Lyle W. A Passion for Souls: The Life of D.L. Moody. Chicago: Moody Publishers, 2003.

Bibliography

Green, Melody, and David Hazard. No Compromise: The Life Story of Keith Green. Chatsworth, California: Sparrow, 1989.

Lee, Jarena. Religious Experience and Journal of Mrs. Jarena Lee, Pantianos Classics, 1836.

McGaw, Francis. John Hyde: The Apostle of Prayer. Minneapolis: Bethany House, 1970.

Metaxas, Eric. Amazing Grace: William Wilberforce and the Heroic Campaign to End Slavery. New York: Harper Collins, 2007.

Metaxas, Eric. Martin Luther: The Man Who Rediscovered God and Changed the World. New York: Penguin Books, 2017.

Metaxas, Eric. Seven Women: And the Secret of Their Greatness. Nashville: Nelson Books, 2015.

Miller, Basil. William Carey: The Father of Modern Missions. Bethany House, 1980.

Nee, Watchman. The Normal Christian Life: Carol Stream, Illinois: Tyndale, 1977.

Palau, Luis and Paul J. Pastor. Palau: A Life on Fire. Grand Rapids: Zondervan, 2019.

Palau, Luis. Where is God When Bad Things Happen: Finding Solace in Times of Trouble. New York: Doubleday, 1999.

Palau: The Movie (the biographical film), thepalaumovie.com, directed by Kevin Knoblock, 2019.

Paton, John. Missionary Patriarch: The True Story of John G. Paton. Vision Forum, 2001.

Peterson, Carla L. Doers of the Word: African American Women Speakers and Writers in the North (1830–1880). New Brunswick, New Jersey: Rutgers University Press, 1998.

Skinner, Betty Lee. Daws: The Story of Dawson Trotman, Founder of The Navigators. Grand Rapids: Zondervan, 1974.

Swift, Catherine. Eric Liddell. Minneapolis: Bethany, 1990.

Taylor, Howard and Geraldine. Hudson Taylor's Spiritual Secret. Chicago: Moody Publishers, 2009.

Taylor, J. Hudson. The Autobiography of J. Hudson Taylor. Pantianos Classics, 1894.

MORE RECOMMENDED READING

Andrews, Mary Raymond Shipman. A Lost Commander: Florence Nightingale. New York: Doubleday, 1929.

Belmonte, Kevin. William Wilberforce. Colorado Springs: NavPress, 2002.

Benge, Janet & Geoff. George Müller: The Guardian of Bristol's Orphans. Seattle: YWAM, 1999.

Brown, Pam. Florence Nightingale. Milwaukee: Gareth Stevens, 1989.

Day of Discovery: The Biography of Josiah Henson. Dir. Don Boyer. 60 min. RBC Ministries, 2005. Videocassette.

Elliot, Elisabeth. A Chance to Die: The Life and Legacy of Amy Carmichael. Grand Rapids: Baker, 1987.

Furneaux, Robin. William Wilberforce. London: Hamish Hamilton, 1974.

Galli, Mark, and Ted Olsen. 131 Christians Everyone Should Know. Nashville: Broadman & Holman, 2000.

George, Timothy. Faithful Witness: The Life and Mission of William Carey. Birmingham, Alabama: New Hope, 1991.

Grubb, Norman. C.T. Studd: Cricketer and Pioneer. Fort Washington, Pennsylvania: Christian Literature Crusade, 1994.

More Recommended Reading

Harmon, Rebecca Lamar. Susanna, Mother of the Wesleys. Nashville: Abingdon, 1968.

Henson, Josiah. Father Henson's Story of His Own Life. Boston: Jewett, 1858.

Laurent, Bob. Watchman Nee: Man of Suffering. Ulrichsville, Ohio: Barbour, 1998.

McReynolds, Kathy. Susanna Wesley. Minneapolis: Bethany, 1998.

Müller, George. The Life of Trust: Being a Narrative of the Lord's Dealings with George Müller. New York: Sheldon and Company, 1878.

Newton, John A. Susanna Wesley and the Puritan Tradition in Methodism. Werrington, Great Britain: Epworth Press, 2002.

Reccord, Bob, and Randy Singer. Made to Count. Nashville: W Publishing, 2004.

Watchman Nee. Living Stream Ministry. 2002. Available: www.watchmannee.org. July 2004.

Wellman, Sam. William Carey: Father of Modern Missions. Uhrichsville, Ohio: Barbour, 1997.

FORGE RESOURCES & CONNECTION

Forge Books and Resources
ForgeForward.org/Resources

Forge Speakers and Events
ForgeForward.org/Speakers

Forge Equipping Programs
ForgeForward.org/Equipping

Contact Us
ForgeForward.org
303.745.8191
info@forgeforward.org

Forge: Kingdom Building Ministries
14485 E Evans Avenue
Denver, Colorado 80014

Ordinary people everywhere are joining God's extraordinary Kingdom harvest movement. It's your turn. Are you ready to get laboring?

Made in the USA
Middletown, DE
11 May 2021